NERO

NÉRON

Cinq oculin.

NERO

Elizabeth Powers

CHELSEA HOUSE PUBLISHERS
NEW YORK
NEW HAVEN   PHILADELPHIA

EDITOR-IN-CHIEF: Nancy Toff
EXECUTIVE EDITOR: Remmel T. Nunn
MANAGING EDITOR: Karyn Gullen Browne
COPY CHIEF: Juliann Barbato
PICTURE EDITOR: Adrian G. Allen
ART DIRECTOR: Giannella Garrett
MANUFACTURING MANAGER: Gerald Levine

Staff for NERO:

SENIOR EDITOR: John W. Selfridge
ASSISTANT EDITOR: Kathleen McDermott
COPY EDITOR: Terrance Dolan
EDITORIAL ASSISTANT: Sean Ginty
ASSOCIATE PICTURE EDITOR: Juliette Dickstein
PICTURE RESEARCHER: Linda Peer
SENIOR DESIGNER: David Murray
ASSISTANT DESIGNER: Jill Goldreyer
PRODUCTION COORDINATOR: Joseph Romano
COVER ILLUSTRATION: Joe Ciardiello

CREATIVE DIRECTOR: Harold Steinberg

3 5 7 9 8 6 4 2

Library of Congress Cataloging in Publication Data

Powers, Elizabeth, 1944–
NERO.

(World leaders past and present)
Bibliography: p.
Includes index.
1. Nero, Emperor of Rome, 37–68. 2. Rome—History—Nero,
54–68. 3. Roman emperors—Biography. I. Title. II. Series:
World leaders past & present.
DG285.P69   1988   937'.07'0924 [B]   87-24918

ISBN 0-87754-544-8

Contents

John Adams
John Quincy Adams
Konrad Adenauer
Alexander the Great
Salvador Allende
Marc Antony
Corazon Aquino
Yasir Arafat
King Arthur
Hafez al-Assad
Kemal Atatürk
Attila
Clement Attlee
Augustus Caesar
Menachem Begin
David Ben-Gurion
Otto von Bismarck
Léon Blum
Simon Bolívar
Cesare Borgia
Willy Brandt
Leonid Brezhnev
Julius Caesar
John Calvin
Jimmy Carter
Fidel Castro
Catherine the Great
Charlemagne
Chiang Kai-Shek
Winston Churchill
Georges Clemenceau
Cleopatra
Constantine the Great
Hernán Cortés
Oliver Cromwell
Georges-Jacques
   Danton
Jefferson Davis
Moshe Dayan
Charles de Gaulle
Eamon De Valera
Eugene Debs
Deng Xiaoping
Benjamin Disraeli
Alexander Dubček
François & Jean-Claude
   Duvalier
Dwight Eisenhower
Eleanor of Aquitaine
Elizabeth I
Faisal
Ferdinand & Isabella
Francisco Franco
Benjamin Franklin

Frederick the Great
Indira Gandhi
Mohandas Gandhi
Giuseppe Garibaldi
Amin & Bashir Gemayel
Genghis Khan
William Gladstone
Mikhail Gorbachev
Ulysses S. Grant
Ernesto "Che" Guevara
Tenzin Gyatso
Alexander Hamilton
Dag Hammarskjöld
Henry VIII
Henry of Navarre
Paul von Hindenburg
Hirohito
Adolf Hitler
Ho Chi Minh
King Hussein
Ivan the Terrible
Andrew Jackson
James I
Wojciech Jaruzelski
Thomas Jefferson
Joan of Arc
Pope John XXIII
Pope John Paul II
Lyndon Johnson
Benito Juárez
John Kennedy
Robert Kennedy
Jomo Kenyatta
Ayatollah Khomeini
Nikita Khrushchev
Kim Il Sung
Martin Luther King, Jr.
Henry Kissinger
Kublai Khan
Lafayette
Robert E. Lee
Vladimir Lenin
Abraham Lincoln
David Lloyd George
Louis XIV
Martin Luther
Judas Maccabeus
James Madison
Nelson & Winnie
   Mandela
Mao Zedong
Ferdinand Marcos
George Marshall

Mary, Queen of Scots
Tomáš Masaryk
Golda Meir
Klemens von Metternich
James Monroe
Hosni Mubarak
Robert Mugabe
Benito Mussolini
Napoléon Bonaparte
Gamal Abdel Nasser
Jawaharlal Nehru
Nero
Nicholas II
Richard Nixon
Kwame Nkrumah
Daniel Ortega
Mohammed Reza Pahlavi
Thomas Paine
Charles Stewart
   Parnell
Pericles
Juan Perón
Peter the Great
Pol Pot
Muammar el-Qaddafi
Ronald Reagan
Cardinal Richelieu
Maximilien Robespierre
Eleanor Roosevelt
Franklin Roosevelt
Theodore Roosevelt
Anwar Sadat
Haile Selassie
Prince Sihanouk
Jan Smuts
Joseph Stalin
Sukarno
Sun Yat-sen
Tamerlane
Mother Teresa
Margaret Thatcher
Josip Broz Tito
Toussaint L'Ouverture
Leon Trotsky
Pierre Trudeau
Harry Truman
Queen Victoria
Lech Walesa
George Washington
Chaim Weizmann
Woodrow Wilson
Xerxes
Emiliano Zapata
Zhou Enlai

CHELSEA HOUSE PUBLISHERS

ON LEADERSHIP

Arthur M. Schlesinger, jr.

LEADERSHIP, it may be said, is really what makes the world go round. Love no doubt smooths the passage; but love is a private transaction between consenting adults. Leadership is a public transaction with history. The idea of leadership affirms the capacity of individuals to move, inspire, and mobilize masses of people so that they act together in pursuit of an end. Sometimes leadership serves good purposes, sometimes bad; but whether the end is benign or evil, great leaders are those men and women who leave their personal stamp on history.

Now, the very concept of leadership implies the proposition that individuals can make a difference. This proposition has never been universally accepted. From classical times to the present day, eminent thinkers have regarded individuals as no more than the agents and pawns of larger forces, whether the gods and goddesses of the ancient world or, in the modern era, race, class, nation, the dialectic, the will of the people, the spirit of the times, history itself. Against such forces, the individual dwindles into insignificance.

So contends the thesis of historical determinism. Tolstoy's great novel *War and Peace* offers a famous statement of the case. Why, Tolstoy asked, did millions of men in the Napoleonic Wars, denying their human feelings and their common sense, move back and forth across Europe slaughtering their fellows? "The war," Tolstoy answered, "was bound to happen simply because it was bound to happen." All prior history predetermined it. As for leaders, they, Tolstoy said, "are but the labels that serve to give a name to an end and, like labels, they have the least possible connection with the event." The greater the leader, "the more conspicuous the inevitability and the predestination of every act he commits." The leader, said Tolstoy, is "the slave of history."

Determinism takes many forms. Marxism is the determinism of class. Nazism the determinism of race. But the idea of men and women as the slaves of history runs athwart the deepest human instincts. Rigid determinism abolishes the idea of human freedom—

the assumption of free choice that underlies every move we make, every word we speak, every thought we think. It abolishes the idea of human responsibility, since it is manifestly unfair to reward or punish people for actions that are by definition beyond their control. No one can live consistently by any deterministic creed. The Marxist states prove this themselves by their extreme susceptibility to the cult of leadership.

More than that, history refutes the idea that individuals make no difference. In December 1931 a British politician crossing Park Avenue in New York City between 76th and 77th Streets around 10:30 P.M. looked in the wrong direction and was knocked down by an automobile—a moment, he later recalled, of a man aghast, a world aglare: "I do not understand why I was not broken like an eggshell or squashed like a gooseberry." Fourteen months later an American politician, sitting in an open car in Miami, Florida, was fired on by an assassin; the man beside him was hit. Those who believe that individuals make no difference to history might well ponder whether the next two decades would have been the same had Mario Constasino's car killed Winston Churchill in 1931 and Giuseppe Zangara's bullet killed Franklin Roosevelt in 1933. Suppose, in addition, that Adolf Hitler had been killed in the street fighting during the Munich *Putsch* of 1923 and that Lenin had died of typhus during World War I. What would the 20th century be like now?

For better or for worse, individuals do make a difference. "The notion that a people can run itself and its affairs anonymously," wrote the philosopher William James, "is now well known to be the silliest of absurdities. Mankind does nothing save through initiatives on the part of inventors, great or small, and imitation by the rest of us—these are the sole factors in human progress. Individuals of genius show the way, and set the patterns, which common people then adopt and follow."

Leadership, James suggests, means leadership in thought as well as in action. In the long run, leaders in thought may well make the greater difference to the world. But, as Woodrow Wilson once said, "Those only are leaders of men, in the general eye, who lead in action. . . . It is at their hands that new thought gets its translation into the crude language of deeds." Leaders in thought often invent in solitude and obscurity, leaving to later generations the tasks of imitation. Leaders in action—the leaders portrayed in this series—have to be effective in their own time.

And they cannot be effective by themselves. They must act in response to the rhythms of their age. Their genius must be adapted, in a phrase of William James's, "to the receptivities of the moment." Leaders are useless without followers. "There goes the mob," said the French politician hearing a clamor in the streets. "I am their leader. I must follow them." Great leaders turn the inchoate emotions of the mob to purposes of their own. They seize on the opportunities of their time, the hopes, fears, frustrations, crises, potentialities. They succeed when events have prepared the way for them, when the community is awaiting to be aroused, when they can provide the clarifying and organizing ideas. Leadership ignites the circuit between the individual and the mass and thereby alters history.

It may alter history for better or for worse. Leaders have been responsible for the most extravagant follies and most monstrous crimes that have beset suffering humanity. They have also been vital in such gains as humanity has made in individual freedom, religious and racial tolerance, social justice, and respect for human rights.

There is no sure way to tell in advance who is going to lead for good and who for evil. But a glance at the gallery of men and women in *World Leaders—Past and Present* suggests some useful tests.

One test is this: Do leaders lead by force or by persuasion? By command or by consent? Through most of history leadership was exercised by the divine right of authority. The duty of followers was to defer and to obey. "Theirs not to reason why / Theirs but to do and die." On occasion, as with the so-called enlightened despots of the 18th century in Europe, absolutist leadership was animated by humane purposes. More often, absolutism nourished the passion for domination, land, gold, and conquest and resulted in tyranny.

The great revolution of modern times has been the revolution of equality. The idea that all people should be equal in their legal condition has undermined the old structure of authority, hierarchy, and deference. The revolution of equality has had two contrary effects on the nature of leadership. For equality, as Alexis de Tocqueville pointed out in his great study *Democracy in America*, might mean equality in servitude as well as equality in freedom.

"I know of only two methods of establishing equality in the political world," Tocqueville wrote. "Rights must be given to every citizen, or none at all to anyone . . . save one, who is the master of all." There was no middle ground "between the sovereignty of all and the absolute power of one man." In his astonishing prediction

of 20th-century totalitarian dictatorship, Tocqueville explained how the revolution of equality could lead to the *"Führerprinzip"* and more terrible absolutism than the world had ever known.

But when rights are given to every citizen and the sovereignty of all is established, the problem of leadership takes a new form, becomes more exacting than ever before. It is easy to issue commands and enforce them by the rope and the stake, the concentration camp and the *gulag.* It is much harder to use argument and achievement to overcome opposition and win consent. The Founding Fathers of the United States understood the difficulty. They believed that history had given them the opportunity to decide, as Alexander Hamilton wrote in the first Federalist Paper, whether men are indeed capable of basing government on "reflection and choice, or whether they are forever destined to depend . . . on accident and force."

Government by reflection and choice called for a new style of leadership and a new quality of followership. It required leaders to be responsive to popular concerns, and it required followers to be active and informed participants in the process. Democracy does not eliminate emotion from politics; sometimes it fosters demagoguery; but it is confident that, as the greatest of democratic leaders put it, you cannot fool all of the people all of the time. It measures leadership by results and retires those who overreach or falter or fail.

It is true that in the long run despots are measured by results too. But they can postpone the day of judgment, sometimes indefinitely, and in the meantime they can do infinite harm. It is also true that democracy is no guarantee of virtue and intelligence in government, for the voice of the people is not necessarily the voice of God. But democracy, by assuring the right of opposition, offers built-in resistance to the evils inherent in absolutism. As the theologian Reinhold Niebuhr summed it up, "Man's capacity for justice makes democracy possible, but man's inclination to injustice makes democracy necessary."

A second test for leadership is the end for which power is sought. When leaders have as their goal the supremacy of a master race or the promotion of totalitarian revolution or the acquisition and exploitation of colonies or the protection of greed and privilege or the preservation of personal power, it is likely that their leadership will do little to advance the cause of humanity. When their goal is the abolition of slavery, the liberation of women, the enlargement of opportunity for the poor and powerless, the extension of equal rights to racial minorities, the defense of the freedoms of expression and opposition, it is likely that their leadership will increase the sum of human liberty and welfare.

Leaders have done great harm to the world. They have also conferred great benefits. You will find both sorts in this series. Even "good" leaders must be regarded with a certain wariness. Leaders are not demigods; they put on their trousers one leg after another just like ordinary mortals. No leader is infallible, and every leader needs to be reminded of this at regular intervals. Irreverence irritates leaders but is their salvation. Unquestioning submission corrupts leaders and demeans followers. Making a cult of a leader is always a mistake. Fortunately hero worship generates its own antidote. "Every hero," said Emerson, "becomes a bore at last."

The signal benefit the great leaders confer is to embolden the rest of us to live according to our own best selves, to be active, insistent, and resolute in affirming our own sense of things. For great leaders attest to the reality of human freedom against the supposed inevitabilities of history. And they attest to the wisdom and power that may lie within the most unlikely of us, which is why Abraham Lincoln remains the supreme example of great leadership. A great leader, said Emerson, exhibits new possibilities to all humanity. "We feed on genius. . . . Great men exist that there may be greater men."

Great leaders, in short, justify themselves by emancipating and empowering their followers. So humanity struggles to master its destiny, remembering with Alexis de Tocqueville: "It is true that around every man a fatal circle is traced beyond which he cannot pass; but within the wide verge of that circle he is powerful and free; as it is with man, so with communities."

1

A Roman Holiday

Hail, Emperor! Greetings from men who are about to die!" The day's fighters, standing in the center of the amphitheater — the huge arena that held the gladiatorial contests — extended their right arms and addressed the standard cry to the central figure in the gilded imperial box. The three tiers of the amphitheater were filled with people, perhaps as many as 45,000, some of whom had lined up the night before for free seats. At the gladiators' words, the crowd roared its approval for young Nero Claudius Caesar Drusus Germanicus, emperor of Rome.

Seated on the cushioned *pulvinar* — the emperor's couch — and surrounded by a vast retinue of retainers and slaves, the emperor acknowledged the cheers reaching his ears from all sides. Nero was not a tall man and was already becoming corpulent. In addition, he was nearsighted and relied on a cut emerald, which he used as a magnifier, to watch the gladiators below him. As he signaled for the games to begin, the Romans settled back to enjoy a full day of bloody combat. Each spectator had a favorite fighter, and bets had been waged. This was the greatest amusement available to the common people of Rome, and they reveled in the passions it aroused.

> *The amphitheater was strictly a place where human sacrifice was carried out for the amusement and titillation of the populace.*
> —BARRY CUNLIFFE
> British historian

A fresco from Pompeii shows a gladiatorial contest in a Roman amphitheater. Although the games were not originally for public viewing, by the reign of Nero in the mid-1st century A.D. they were a hugely popular spectator sport.

The gladiators had arrived in chariots, from which they had stepped down to complete the militarylike march around the inside circle of the arena. As the fighters, dressed in short, sleeveless tunics draped with cloaks dyed purple and embroidered with gold, paraded in the amphitheater, slaves carrying the gladiatorial weapons followed them. Most of the gladiators in fact were slaves, criminals, or prisoners of war, sometimes from the far reaches of the empire — fair-haired Germans, tall, powerful Celts, black-skinned Africans. Some, however, were Roman citizens or freedmen who, because they had squandered their family fortunes or perhaps simply had a lust for battle, signed up voluntarily with the gladiatorial trainers.

The word *gladiator* comes from the Latin *gladius*, meaning "sword." It is likely that the ancient Romans borrowed the custom from the neighboring Etruscans, who staged gladiatorial contests as funeral games, perhaps using the victims as sacrifices to the blood thirst of the dead. The earliest recorded Roman gladiatorial show took place in 264 B.C. in Rome, and the event quickly grew in popularity. Under Julius Caesar, in the 1st century B.C., gladiators fought for the public's amusement. By the time of Nero, a century later, the contests were an enormously popular spectator sport that had made superstars of the best fighters.

A Roman mosaic portrays some of the different types of gladiators. Often the trained gladiators fought convicted criminals or wild beasts brought from all over the Roman Empire.

A gladiatorial helmet bears figures representing Rome and the provinces. Fighters were armed differently to increase the variety and excitement of the combat.

Gladiators were trained in special schools called *ludi*, the greatest of which was the *Ludus Magnus* — the Great School — in Rome. Because of their training and their low status in life, the gladiators were considered potentially dangerous men and were carefully guarded. Ruins of a gladiatorial school in the city of Pompeii indicate that the fighters were kept in leg irons when not in the arena. For fear of suicide, the authorities forbade real weapons at the training centers; the gladiators practiced with wooden swords.

To make sure the fight was fair, the gladiators were chosen before the games in public, by lot. There were several different types, including Samnites with plumed, visored helmets and oblong shields; *myrmillones*, so called from the symbol of a myrmillo, a type of fish, on their helmets; the Thracians, who wore greaves to protect both legs and carried curved daggers; *laquearii*, who lassoed their opponents; *retiarii*, who were unarmed except for the nets with which they snared their opponents and the tridents they used to finish them off; and

The Colosseum in Rome was the greatest of the ancient Roman amphitheaters. The fighters and wild beasts stayed in small, dank rooms under the central floor until their turn came to perform. They then entered through a great arch opposite the imperial box.

the fully armed *secutores*. The day began in mock combat with wooden swords to warm up the fighters. At length, a *tuba* — the Romans' straight war trumpet — rang out to announce that the real fighting with sharp weapons was about to start. To the accompaniment of horns and flutes, which may have provided music throughout the day, the first contest began.

The gladiators' trainer had reminded his fighters the evening before the games that anyone could win, but only the best gladiators knew the art of dying. The first pair of gladiators would present the spectacle of a retiarius and a *noxius*, the Latin name for a condemned felon. The schools could not turn out fighters fast enough; the felons were included in order to replenish the constantly dwindling ranks of fighters. The noxii were armed with only a small shield and dagger. The noxius, of course, would be terrified — for he was not a trained fighter — at being trapped and hunted down like a wild animal.

When the retiarius approached and tried to fling the net over the head of the noxius, the latter did what many had done before him: He turned on his heel and ran. As he did so the boos of the spectators filled the warm Roman air. Above all, the crowd hated cowardly displays, and often shouts of "Whip him, kill him, burn him!" would be heard for a less than aggressive fighter. A man holding a red-hot branding iron stood at the edge of the arena to force any unwilling fighter back into the arms of his opponent. As the contest was being decided in the arena, the crowd could hear the sounds of swords being sharpened in preparation for the next fight.

The retiarius stalked forward with slow, deliberate movements. The net, which had a cord attached to enable its retrieval, sailed toward the noxius and ensnared him. The retiarius struck the man with his trident. The victor waved his bloody trident in the air, but the crowd, never shy at protesting what it considered a poor spectacle, booed him, too.

When the attendant carrying the mallet rushed up, Nero turned away. This was one part of the entertainment he did not relish — seeing the vanquished man pounded on the forehead to make sure he was dead. Nero considered himself an artist; because of his sensitive nature, he did not like the relentless killing that went on at the games. Early in his reign he had sought to prohibit bloodshed in the arena, but he was forced to give up his idea when faced with the intensity of the popular opposition. The body was dragged away, and another attendant sprinkled sand, or the colored (red or blue-green) dust that Nero favored, on the ground to cover the blood.

In this drawing, based on a Roman relief, the gladiator kneeling at left raises a finger to ask for a pardon. The fighter at right, denied a pardon, loses his life. Crowd favorites were often spared to fight another time.

As the fights continued, Nero was acutely aware of the crowd's pulse. Because of his weak eyes, he relied on spies to report on whose applause was halfhearted and on which members of the Senate, Rome's ruling body, were not present at the games to show their respect. Nero seldom let pass an opportunity to appear generous to the common people, however, and during the contests he would motion to one of his retainers to distribute tokens for meat, grain, and clothes to the more raucous parts of the crowd.

A fast-paced, thrilling match made the crowd's pulse race, and supporters of one or the other fighter sprang to their feet to scream out encouragement. Cheering sections developed as hand-to-hand combat became fierce. Bets were placed on who would survive the match. When a gladiator was struck down but not mortally wounded, he could ask for mercy from the emperor by lifting a forefinger.

If the gladiator had demonstrated remarkable courage, the crowd was on his side. The wooden structure of the amphitheater would tremble and sway from the stomping of feet, and the musicians would respond with brass to the cries. Then the *procurator a muneribus* stalked out to the center of the arena. It was this man's job to determine the fate of the fallen gladiator. He usually deferred to the multitude. If the crowd liked the gladiator, the entire amphitheater was a sea of waving white handkerchiefs, a sign to spare the gladiator for another day's fighting. If the procurator saw a generous number of thumbs turned down, the victor stood ready to deal the vanquished a mortal blow. The procurator turned to the emperor for the final judgment.

A hush descended momentarily in the vast amphitheater as all eyes turned to the emperor. Nero relished the spotlight and did not refrain from a little theatrical performance. He cast a disdainful glance at the wide terrace above the arena where the senators sat, though his weak eyes probably only made out their bright white togas. His eyes traveled

up to the top tier, where the poor stood in their drab, gray clothes. The arena was their parliament, and Nero respected the power of the mob. He would not go against the wishes of the crowd. By the time Nero turned his thumb up, the people were in a frenzy of enthusiasm for their young emperor.

It was the support of these people that granted Nero the power of life and death in the arena. He extended this power to the entire realm. By the end of Nero's reign, the bewildered emperor would find himself on the losing end of the much vaster game of politics in the Roman Empire.

Nero rejects a gladiator's request for a pardon by turning his thumb down. Nero always gauged the emotions of the clamoring crowd before making a judgment on the fate of a fighter.

2

The Young Nero

At the time of Nero's birth in A.D. 37, the Roman Empire had not yet reached its greatest extent, but it encompassed a vast amount of territory surrounding the Mediterranean Sea. Roman provinces included modern Spain, France, Belgium, Italy, Greece, southern England, North Africa, and parts of central and eastern Europe, Turkey, and the Middle East. In the mid-1st century A.D. the empire enjoyed prosperity and stability under the *pax Romana* — the Roman peace — established by Rome's first emperor, Augustus, who reigned from the mid-1st century B.C. to the early years of the 1st century A.D.

Rome began around 753 B.C. as a small settlement on one of the Seven Hills of that city, but it soon distinguished itself from its neighbors. Between 241 B.C., when Rome acquired the island of Sicily after a 20-year war with the Carthaginians of North Africa, and A.D. 43, when Nero's predecessor, his uncle Claudius, annexed the south of England, Rome built the most extensive empire the world had yet known.

He had never had to work, had never commanded an army or held an administrative post, never previously felt responsibility, never enjoyed the discipline of limited or delegated power.
—ALLAN MASSIE
British historian, on young Nero

The young Nero stands at the foot of his mother, Agrippina the Younger. Nero had a difficult childhood: His father died early, his mother was exiled, and he was sent to live with an aunt who kept him in poverty.

Augustus, the grandnephew of Julius Caesar, was the first emperor of Rome. His family, the Julio-Claudians, ruled the empire until Nero's death, which ended the dynasty.

The backbone of imperial strength was the Roman army. Roman soldiers, called legionaries, were posted in every province to maintain order and ensure local compliance with Roman law. By Nero's time, the majority of the soldiers in the Roman army were drawn from the provinces. It was not uncommon for a soldier from Syria to find himself posted on the Danube in Germany or in Britain.

Under the pax Romana commerce flourished throughout the empire. The extensive system of roads built by the Romans connected the various parts of the empire, enabling easy movement by both people and goods. Pottery made in Italy might be used by peasants in northern France. Africa supplied two-thirds of Rome's grain, and Spain contributed minerals. Perfumes, rare woods, and silks

from the East were brought by traders to the cities of the empire: Rome, of course, but also Alexandria in Egypt, Trier in Germany, Nîmes in France, Bath in England, Palmyra in Syria, Carnuntum on the Danube. In the 1st century A.D. all these cities contained Roman temples and baths, arches, fora (open public squares), theaters, markets, and colonnaded streets. Roman villas with heated rooms and colorful wall and floor mosaics dotted the countrysides of Spain, Africa, the Black Sea region, and southern England.

Rome, the city at the center of this world, boasted a population of about 1 million inhabitants. It had sewers, running water, and good roads. A truly cosmopolitan city, it provided its citizens with many services and goods. There were fishwives and pastry cooks, booksellers and purveyors of wine, gladiator trainers and chemists, shoemakers and ironmongers, money changers and rent collectors.

Romans also lived with the evils that accompany prosperity, chief among them being 150,000 poor people, many from the Italian countryside who had given up farming, and many former slaves, all of whom lived in crowded tenements and had no fixed occupation. These people were known as the *plebs* — the Roman "mob" — and it was the policy of the

This carved sarcophagus shows Romans fighting barbarians. Rome's greatness originated in the tremendous power of its army, and no emperor could rule without the support of the military.

The Romans expanded their empire along a vast system of roads built in straight lines to allow easy, fast transportation for the army. The Appian Way, from Rome to Brundisium on the east coast, is one of many Roman roads still in use.

emperors to provide this unpredictable group with "bread and circuses" — free bread dole and the amusements of the amphitheater — to keep it content. Roman history abounded with tales of the destruction the mob could wreak when aroused, and it was a foolish ruler who imperiled his standing with this class.

Such was the world Nero was born into on December 15, A.D. 37. He was a member of the Julio-Claudian dynasty with ties to both Julius Caesar, the first ruler of Rome after the fall of the Roman republic in the 1st century B.C., and Augustus. Nero's father, Gnaeus Domitius Ahenobarbus (the final name means "bronze bearded"), was descended from an old and noble Roman family related to Marc Antony and Julius Caesar. Despite such eminence at its roots, the family possessed more than its share of vices. Nero's own father was known for his dishonesty, corruption, and drunkenness. According to the Roman biographer and historian Gaius Suetonius Tranquillus, Gnaeus ran down and killed a boy on the main road to Rome, and he once gouged out the eyes of a man who spoke his mind too freely.

Nero was blessed on his mother's side as well with an eminent, though sordid, ancestry. His mother, Julia Agrippina (known as Agrippina the Younger), was the daughter of the great general and popular hero Germanicus (Nero Claudius Drusus), the grandnephew of Augustus. After the death of Germanicus in A.D. 19, however, his family was exiled by Emperor Tiberius, the brother of Germanicus. Germanicus's widow, Agrippina the Elder, suffered such degrading and cruel treatment in exile — she was blinded in one eye after being struck by a soldier — that she starved herself to death. Two of Agrippina the Younger's brothers died squalid deaths; one committed suicide after he was sentenced to die and another was imprisoned and ate the stuffing of his mattress for food before he was finally executed in A.D. 33.

The future emperor Nero was born Lucius Domitius Ahenobarbus, nine months after Tiberius's death and in the year his mother's remaining brother, Gaius, known as Caligula, became emperor. Nero's natal (birth) horoscope prompted various predictions, none of them favorable. According to Suetonius, Nero's father commented that any child born to him and Agrippina was "bound to have a detestable nature and become a public danger."

Under the *pax Romana* of the 1st century A.D., Roman civilization extended from Britain and Spain in the west to Syria and Egypt in the east. This Roman bath is located in Bath, England.

When Nero was three, his father died. Though Nero should have received a large inheritance, Caligula seized the fortune and sent Agrippina into exile on charges of conspiracy against him. Nero was sent to live with his father's sister, Domitia Lepida, who, Suetonius reports, kept the child in dire poverty, giving him a dancer and a barber for companions and tutors.

Caligula, who was rumored to have speeded up his accession to the throne by murdering Tiberius, proved a disastrous ruler. Probably insane, the young emperor indulged in nearly every vice imaginable, capping his bizarre behavior by forcing his sister Drusilla to leave her husband and live incestuously with him as the imperial consort. Caligula's abuse of power finally reached the stage where the Roman senators could tolerate it no longer. Caligula

Caligula, Nero's uncle, demonstrated such personal excess and abuse of power that the praetorian guard — the emperor's military elite — killed him. Nero needed the support of the praetorians, who had direct access to the emperor, in order to remain in power.

was assassinated in A.D. 41 by his palace guard, whereupon Claudius, brother of Germanicus, became emperor. Claudius promptly revoked Agrippina's banishment, and in one of the strange reversals of fortune that mark Rome's imperial history, Agrippina married Claudius, her uncle, in A.D. 49. In a few years she had gone from being the sister of an emperor to being the wife of one, and she promptly prepared to become the mother of one.

Nero had a good claim to the throne, but he was decidedly not the first in line. Claudius's son from his first marriage, Britannicus, was looked upon as most likely to succeed the emperor. There were also a number of distinguished men in Rome — with ties to Augustus — who had equally good claims. One of these was Lucius Silanus, who was engaged to marry Claudius's daughter Octavia. Agrippina managed to eliminate him when she had one of her allies in the Senate accuse him of incest. Ruined, Silanus committed suicide on January 1, A.D. 49, the very day Agrippina married Claudius.

In A.D. 50 Agrippina succeeded in convincing Claudius to formally adopt Nero as his son. Claudius even went a step further and gave Nero precedence over Britannicus, who was two years younger. Agrippina now had no obstacle save one: Claudius himself.

A Pompeii clothing merchant attracted customers to his shop with this sign detailing the clothmaking process. Rome supported an extensive trading network, and many goods, from simple pottery to exotic eastern spices and perfumes, found their way across the empire.

Agrippina possessed formidable powers of energy, cunning, and determination. As the daughter of Germanicus, she also had a resource that most of her rivals could not count on — the loyalty of the military, whose members revered the memory of the great general. She saw to it that any officers favorable to Britannicus were eliminated, and she constantly brought forward her own supporters. One of these men was Sextus Afranius Burrus, who with Agrippina's help became commander of the praetorian guard. The praetorian guard was an elite corps of soldiers — stationed in Rome and surrounding areas in Italy — that had assumed the main responsibility of protecting the emperor. To be commander of the guard was to hold a powerful, lucrative position.

A bronze sculpture of a girl holding a puppy. The common people, called the *plebs*, were a constant threat to the security of Rome. Every emperor kept them content with supplies of free grain and public entertainments.

To prepare Nero for the accession, Agrippina was determined that he be well educated. After her marriage to Claudius in A.D. 49, she talked the emperor into recalling from exile the senator Lucius Annaeus Seneca, who had gained renown as an orator and philosopher. Seneca had been banished to the island of Corsica in A.D. 41 on charges of adultery with Claudius's niece. Up to this time young Nero had received the standard education for noble Romans from Greek tutors. Among his tutors were two philosophers: Alexander of Aegae and Chaeremon of Alexandria. Another of Nero's earliest teachers, a freedman by the name of Anicetus, would later serve Nero in a very different capacity. Nero studied the usual subjects of mythology and the classical writers, but the most important subject for him to study

This Roman amphitheater in Nimes, France, indicates the extent of the Roman cultural influence throughout the empire. The amusements of the arena were provided for both the Roman soldiers stationed in the area and the local inhabitants.

Emperor Claudius (front left), his first wife, and their two children, Britannicus and Octavia. In A.D. 50 Claudius adopted Nero, giving him precedence over his own son. Three years later Nero married Octavia to ensure his tie to the Claudian line.

was rhetoric. This was apparently the reason Agrippina wanted Seneca's help: If Nero was to be emperor, he had to be eloquent. Perhaps she was affected by the ludicrous speeches of her husband, the emperor Claudius, who had a terrible stutter. Seneca, however, was important in another sense. As a follower of Stoicism, a philosophy that stressed the virtues of wisdom, courage, justice, and temperance, Seneca was in a crucial position to exert a positive influence on his pupil.

The young student already showed a curious nature and an artistic temperament. He liked art, drama, and music, especially singing. He had a passion for horses and kept a set of model ivory horses and charioteers. His education seems to have encompassed a broad spectrum, but Suetonius writes that Agrippina discouraged his learning philosophy, which was considered a Greek discipline, unsuitable for well-bred Romans.

In the year A.D. 53, at the age of 16, Nero was married to his cousin Octavia. It was the crowning achievement for Agrippina, who thus ensured Nero's connection to the Augustan line. However, the event was not regarded happily by all. Narcissus, a former Greek slave who had become Claudius's leading adviser, understood Agrippina's intent and sought to influence Claudius against her. Agrippina, aware of this, knew she had little time to lose.

Whether Agrippina actually murdered Claudius is impossible to ascertain. Documents for this period are scant, but both Suetonius and the late 1st–early 2nd-century A.D. Roman historian Tacitus, author of the *Histories* and the *Annals*, and the main historical source for Nero's reign, support such a version of the unfortunate emperor's death. In A.D. 54, Agrippina, taking advantage of Claudius's notorious gluttony, poisoned a dish of mushrooms, his favorite food. Tacitus describes the almost comic end of the emperor: "But because Claudius was torpid — or drunk — its effect was not at first apparent; and an evacuation of his bowels seemed to have saved him. Agrippina was horrified. . . . She had already secured the complicity of the emperor's doctor Xenophon; and now she called him in. The story is that, while pretending to help Claudius to vomit, he put a feather dipped in a quick poison down his throat."

Before the Senate could propose a new emperor, Agrippina was busy creating her own. Burrus, the praetorian commander, stationed troops in the palace to prevent Britannicus from leaving. At an auspicious hour forecast by astrologers, Burrus led Nero to the praetorian guards' camp, where the 17-year-old youth was acclaimed emperor. The Senate, which recognized the soldiers' power to back any candidate they wanted, assented.

Agrippina's machinations had been an overwhelming success: Nero was the new emperor. Agrippina had taught Nero that *anyone* who stood in the way of one's desires was expendable. As emperor, Nero would demonstrate to his domineering mother that he had learned his lessons well.

In public, Agrippina was austere and often arrogant. Her private life was chaste— unless power was to be gained. Her passion to acquire money was unbounded. She wanted it as a stepping stone to supremacy.
—TACITUS
Roman historian

3

On the Throne

Nero, whose principal interests were horses and singing, had no experience in running an empire. Yet so many good actions are attributed to Nero in the first years of his reign that it seems the young emperor tried very hard to be a just, good leader. One of Nero's first acts was to deify — to give the status of a god to — Claudius, who was the first emperor to receive this honor since Augustus. In doing this, Nero may have astutely aimed at pleasing the army, which had supported Claudius. It was also an obvious attempt to win more status for himself —he was now the son of a god.

In his accession speech to the Senate, Nero paid tribute to that ancient body and promised respect for its privileges and powers. After the reign of Claudius, under whom many senators and equestrians had been persecuted, Nero's apparent sincerity in wishing to work with the Senate and listen to its advice received an enthusiastic welcome. (The equestrian order, the class between the noble senators and the plebs, took its name from the Latin word for horse, *equus*, because it had originally

On the day of his accession the password he gave to the colonel on duty was "The Best of Mothers"; and [Agrippina] and he often rode out together through the streets in her litter.
—SUETONIUS
Roman historian,
on Nero's early days
as emperor

A Roman couple dines in the traditional way, reclining on couches. When Nero became emperor, he won the favor of upper-class Romans for his insistence on upholding traditional virtues and respecting the position of the Senate.

A mounted officer adorns a tombstone relief. *Equites* were originally cavalry soldiers, but later the class was defined in terms of income. In Nero's time, most equites were wealthy businessmen or administrators.

been the army cavalry. By Nero's time, however, this class was composed primarily of wealthy merchants, administrators, and some army officers.) The 17-year-old emperor, a short, blond youth attired in splendid imperial robes, vowed open and impartial justice and the separation of affairs of state from the business of the imperial household.

The new emperor ruled in such good faith during the first five years of his reign that those years are sometimes referred to as a "golden age." Nero was conscientious in his dealings with the Senate and, in his appointments, filled offices with men of high caliber from senatorial ranks. In his judgment of cases he deliberated slowly and carefully. Ironically, in view of later events, he occasionally opposed capital punishment. Suetonius reports that when called upon to sign execution orders for convicted felons, Nero exclaimed, "How I wish I had never learned to write!" In one case involving a particularly unpleasant official named Marcus Suillius Nerullinus, Nero displayed the moderation of a seasoned judge. Roman custom awarded those prosecuting a man a portion of his estate if the man was found guilty and executed. In their greed, prosecutors

went after Suillius's son, as well; but Nero determined that justice had been done and refused to allow the son's prosecution.

Much of the credit for the moderation and efficiency of the early years of Nero's reign must be attributed to the influence of his advisers Burrus and, especially, Seneca. In A.D. 55, the year after Nero's accession to power, Seneca dedicated his *De Clementia — On Clemency —* to his former pupil. In this work, Seneca laid down the principles for a benevolent reign, hoping that Nero would follow the example. Suetonius wrote that Nero missed no opportunity to be generous and affable. Nero seemed to be content with performing only those governmental duties that were necessary for him to address personally, leaving the daily business of running the empire to Seneca, Burrus, and other advisers. Having been under his mother's domination for years, he was unused to wielding his own power.

Had Nero relied exclusively on the counsel of Seneca and Burrus, he might have become a model ruler. Yet he lived in imperial Rome, where constant intrigue and shuffling for power undermined his good intentions and exposed him to flatterers and others who preyed on his fears. His chief aggravation remained Agrippina. In the first year of her son's reign she exercised a great deal of control. Coins issued in that first year show her profile on the obverse, important side, whereas Nero's graces the reverse. A special chamber was built for Senate deliberations in the palace so that she could listen to the proceedings. This way she could also discover those who consistently disagreed with the emperor and thus might prove to be potential threats to Nero or herself. One rival that Agrippina disposed of soon after Nero's accession was Marcus Junius Silanus, brother of the unlucky Lucius, the former fiancé of Octavia. Agrippina sent an agent to poison Silanus, who was serving as a provincial governor in the east. Tacitus writes, "He [Junius Silanus] was the great-great-grandson of Augustus; that was the cause of his death."

Nero even thought of abolishing all indirect taxes, a veritable boon to humanity. But members of the Senate dissuaded him from this generous impulse.
—TACITUS
Roman historian, on young Nero's idealism

Nero's tutor, the philosopher Seneca, became the young emperor's most important adviser. The fairness and conscientiousness Nero displayed in his early reign has been credited to Seneca's moderating influence.

Seneca and Burrus owed their positions of influence to Agrippina, but both men were now more interested in the security of the empire and in guiding Nero than in catering to the imperial mother's private ambitions. When Nero fell in love with a former slave named Acte, they did not discourage him, despite his marriage to Octavia. Perhaps they judged that the liaison was a harmless one; a freedwoman could never threaten the status of Nero's noble-born wife, Octavia. Part of the acceptance of the affair by Nero's advisers undoubtedly came from their hope that it would lessen Agrippina's influence over him.

Agrippina was outraged at the idea of a former slave as her rival for Nero's attention. She realized that her political station was dependent upon her personal influence over her son, and she was determined to keep a suffocating hold on him. After her first, ferocious response brought no change in Nero's behavior, she tried excessive maternal concern, even offering her own apartment for the lovers' rendezvous. Both tactics alarmed Nero, who was thoroughly familiar with Agrippina's deviousness, and his advisers implored him not to be taken in by her deceptive behavior.

In one of his few attempts at reconciliation, Nero made a gift to his mother of a jeweled robe from the imperial wardrobe, but Agrippina angrily accused him of withholding the rest of the wardrobe, which was rightfully hers, and an uneasy state of suspicion settled between mother and son. The power struggle heated up when Nero dismissed as financial secretary the freedman Pallas, who had been one of Claudius's advisers and had supported his marriage with Agrippina. Pallas's dismissal was a clear signal to Agrippina that Nero at last believed himself to be in control. Any reduction in the number of her supporters lessened Agrippina's power in government, and she reacted with customary vehemence. She vilified everyone connected with Nero, including Seneca and Burrus. Knowing Nero's excessive insecurity, Agrippina prepared her last weapon to retain her influence: She began talking of a plan to

A relief shows Roman slaves
operating a crane to power a
wheel. Roman technology
was very advanced; there is
evidence that Romans even
made use of indoor plumb-
ing. Slaves provided a free,
limitless source of labor.

make 14-year-old Britannicus — Claudius's son and
Octavia's brother — emperor. Her ability to achieve
this was considerable; as the daughter of Germanicus, Agrippina would command a good deal of respect among the soldiers, and she still had many
political allies. This time, however, the imperial
mother apparently went too far. Nero's fear of usur-
pation by Britannicus would propel him into an act
worthy of his scheming mother herself.

Agrippina's talk of deposing Nero frightened the
young emperor immensely. He was, after all, an
adopted intruder. It would be easy enough to rouse
support for Britannicus, who enjoyed the favor of
the people, as was evident at the Saturnalia cele-
bration the previous December. At this festival, Britannicus, called upon by Nero to recite a song,
brought forth a story of how he had been cheated

Juggling was among the myriad public entertainments to be found in Rome. Many of the street performers were Greeks, and Nero greatly admired their seemingly carefree, uncontrolled lives.

of the power that was rightfully his. Britannicus was roundly cheered by the drunken celebrants, and Nero did not forget it. Now that Agrippina threatened to back Britannicus's claims, Nero felt he had no choice. After all, he had been emperor for a year and was decidedly unwilling to put up with the constant threat of a rival with the imposing stature of Claudius's son.

Nero turned to Locusta, the woman who had helped Agrippina poison Claudius. It seems that in an initial attempt on Britannicus's life the poison was not strong enough, and Nero, impatient for immediate results, had Locusta make an extremely strong poison. At an ordinary palace dinner, Nero carried out his clever plan.

Britannicus was seated at a separate table with other young nobles. As slaves served the food, the guests were entertained by singers and clowns. No Roman noble, especially not an imperial prince, would put a crumb in his mouth without first having a servant taste it, so Britannicus naturally had a taster. Nero had thought of a solution to this problem. The young prince, handed a drink that his servant had tasted, complained it was too hot, whereupon water containing the poison was added. The potion was so strong that the unsuspecting Britannicus dropped dead on the spot.

Nero now displayed his growing flair for the theatrical. Lounging on his couch (which is how the Romans dined), he calmly remarked to the frightened assembly of nobles and slaves that Britannicus had long suffered from epileptic seizures, and he would soon revive. He then continued his dinner as everyone present tried to maintain some degree of composure. Octavia knew that she could not even protest the murder of her brother; she realized who the assassin must have been, but accusing the emperor of such a crime would mean certain death. Agrippina too was forced to hold her tongue, and the deed must have frightened her considerably, for it removed her leverage over Nero. Poisoning his stepbrother was evidence that Nero would stop at nothing.

The reaction of Seneca and Burrus to this ruthless murder showed their complete understanding of the politics involved. Their own lives and careers had survived the caprices of three emperors — Seneca remembered all too well his exile by Claudius — and the killing of Britannicus was certainly not the first political murder they had witnessed. Both probably agreed that the empire was jeopardized by two claimants to power. They may not have approved of the deed, but they dealt with the accomplished fact in the best way they knew. They did nothing to force the issue into the open, protecting Nero from accusations. Tacitus claims that Nero's advisers were mollified by the lavish gifts the emperor distributed: "Some were shocked when, at such a juncture, men of ethical pretensions ac-

Britannicus dies after swallowing a deadly poison. Nero, frightened by Agrippina's threat to support Britannicus's claim to the throne, devised a clever scheme to kill him at dinner.

A statuette of a lar, one of the Roman household gods of domestic harmony. Nero, never attracted by traditional Roman religion, did not worship its many gods, some of whom represented devotion to family.

cepted his distribution of town and country mansions like loot. Others thought they had no choice because the emperor, with his guilty conscience, hoped for impunity if he could bind everyone of importance to himself by generous presents."

Britannicus was hastily cremated that same night, and Nero excused the speed by explaining that the Romans had always held simple funerals for those unfortunates who died young. The reaction of the common people seems to have been one of resignation. There had been many power struggles within the imperial families, and Nero was only following in the footsteps of those who had preceded him. By paying out large amounts of money and giving away gifts, Nero succeeded in effectively si-

lencing those who might have objected. All in all, Nero must have been quite satisfied with the deed, which caused him little trouble.

Britannicus's death put Agrippina in a very precarious position. If Nero hoped to frighten his mother into silence, however, he could not have been more mistaken. After the initial shock, she resumed her ambitious schemes. Nero, frightened anew by his mother's apparently limitless energy to plot against him, begged Burrus to murder her. The praetorian commander talked Nero out of this, pointing out that the guard would never commit a crime against any descendant of Germanicus. Agrippina was then accused by a former supporter, Julia Silana, of fomenting rebellion by pushing forward the claims of Rubellius Plautus, another descendant of Augustus. Nero sent Seneca and Burrus to put charges of treason before his mother, who presented such a passionate argument against her involvement in such a wild plot that not only were the charges dropped, but Julia Silana was sent into exile.

Nero had once more been defeated by his mother. Agrippina, for her part, seems to have realized she had narrowly escaped and maintained a low profile during the next two years. During this time, although the responsible government promised by Nero continued with the help of Seneca, Nero was showing signs of wearying of the duties of public life, such as listening to petitions and attending long-winded sessions of the Senate. He increasingly took refuge in his artistic interests. His circle of friends began to include such people as *pantomimi*, male dancers in gold-embroidered tunics and flowing silk robes who performed mime to music. The emperor picked up the habit of prowling the streets of Rome at night with a group of rowdy friends and accosting people, sometimes beating them up or robbing them at knife point. Nero clearly was more interested in pursuing personal entertainment than in ruling the empire, and what kept him entertained was becoming progressively more brutal and depraved.

4

Agrippina's Downfall

The murder of Britannicus demonstrated what Nero was capable of, but Nero himself did not yet know his ultimate potential for deceit and assassination. Despite Seneca and Burrus's refusal to help him eliminate Agrippina, Nero continued to rely on them, and they in turn exerted a rational influence over the emperor. In A.D. 58, however, Nero met a woman who would encourage him in his quest to be rid of his domineering mother.

Poppaea Sabina, the granddaughter of a consul (one of the highest political positions in Rome), was renowned for her physical beauty. She was married to Rufrius Crispinus but soon became the mistress of Marcus Salvius Otho, a confidant of Nero's who had helped the emperor in his affair with Acte. Poppaea was ruthlessly ambitious and saw the advantages of divorcing her husband to marry Otho, who had great access to the emperor. Otho foolishly proceeded to extol Poppaea's virtues to Nero, who saw no reason why he should not have this woman of exceptional beauty. Nero quickly dispatched the hapless Otho as governor to far-off Lusitania (modern Portugal), and Poppaea became the acknowledged mistress of the emperor.

Hearing how offensively Agrippina was speaking of him to friends she had retained, he became convinced that not only was she sneering at his artistic life but also plotting his downfall.
—MICHAEL GRANT
British historian

Four years into his reign, Nero met Poppaea Sabina, a beautiful but utterly immoral woman who encouraged Nero's uglier side. Ruthlessly ambitious, Poppaea urged Nero to divorce his wife, Octavia, and to rid himself of his domineering mother.

A singer adorns a classical Greek vase. Romans regarded Greek culture as effeminate and frivolous, lacking the more manly Roman virtues. Nero's overt love of Greek culture was thus looked upon with disgust and suspicion.

In a line of poetry written by Nero, Poppaea is said to have amber-colored hair. It was also reported that she preserved her complexion by bathing daily in asses' milk. Tacitus summed up the reports on her: "Poppaea had every asset except goodness. From her mother, the loveliest woman of her day, she inherited distinction and beauty. Her wealth, too, was equal to her birth. She was clever and pleasant to talk to. She seemed respectable. But her life was depraved."

Unlike Seneca, who constantly held Nero to a high standard, Poppaea appealed to Nero's weak side. This fearsome woman knew Nero would never divorce the virtuous Octavia as long as Agrippina lived, so she set about provoking Nero against his mother. According to Suetonius, Nero, who by this time needed little encouragement to reduce his mother to dependence, had already expelled her from the palace and deprived her of her imperial bodyguard. He had bribed people to bring lawsuits

against her. Since her fall from favor, however, the relentless Agrippina had continued to sneer at Nero, especially at his burgeoning artistic pursuits and his *philhellenism* (love for things Greek), which she considered effeminate and not befitting the dignity of the emperor of Rome. (Romans in general, even the lower classes, looked down on the Greeks as an undisciplined people only interested in art, literature, and philosophy. Greeks made up most of the actors, singers, and other entertainment artists whom the upper-class Romans considered little better than slaves on the social ladder. Nero's growing interest in the Greeks and their culture, therefore, was looked upon with disdain by many in Rome.)

Under Poppaea's provocations, the emperor gained the courage to do something he had long wanted to do: kill Agrippina. In the annals of murders committed in imperial Rome, few match the ingenious method Nero employed in his first attempt to kill his mother. With so much murder in her life, she was naturally alert to the possibility of assassination. Poison, stabbing, and other traditional methods were considered by Nero and rejected as posing too many dangers. For assistance, Nero turned to Anicetus, one of his childhood tutors. Anicetus, who now commanded the fleet at Misenum, suggested a collapsible ship; one that would fall to pieces at sea and hurl Agrippina to a death by drowning. Such a death would be easily passed off as an accident — the work of the gods. One can imagine that it also appealed to Nero's sense of the melodramatic.

In mid-March of 59, under a pretense of reconciliation, Nero invited Agrippina to celebrate with him the Feast of Minerva, which took place in the coastal town of Baiae. Nero played his part well. At a banquet, he gave Agrippina the place of honor, and such were his filial attentions that the vigilant imperial mother relaxed her guard. Still, when he walked her down to the dock and put her on the boat intended to take her to her death, his behavior was so ingratiating that one wonders why Agrippina was not suspicious. Tacitus wrote, "When she left,

The Roman goddess Minerva was adopted from the Greek Athena, goddess of wisdom. Nero lured Agrippina with an invitation to celebrate a festival in honor of Minerva at the coastal town of Baiae, where he planned to have her killed.

he saw her off, gazing into her eyes and clinging to her. This may have been a final piece of shamming — or perhaps even Nero's brutal heart was affected by his last sight of his mother, going to her death."

The farcical nature of Anicetus's nautical plan may have contributed to its failure. The roof of a section of the boat that had been weighted with lead caved in, like a startling stage effect, instantly killing one of Agrippina's two attendants and causing the boat to sink, but very slowly. Instead of being hurled to a watery death, Agrippina made a gentle descent into the water as the oarsmen threw their weight to one side in an attempt to capsize the boat. Acceronia, Agrippina's remaining attendant, made the fatal mistake of proclaiming herself to be Agrippina. Her reasons for doing so are unclear; perhaps, unaware of the real purpose of the trip, Acceronia felt that the sailors would be more likely to help the imperial mother and so sought to save herself. When

This Roman mosaic shows a boat like the one constructed for Agrippina's "accidental" death. The imperial mother, however, survived the collapse of the weighted roof and swam to safety.

Agrippina feigned ignorance of Nero's plot against her, but Nero, petrified that she would depose him, sent soldiers to kill her at her villa. Nero's matricide was among the most shocking crimes committed by a Roman ruler.

she declared herself to be Agrippina, however, the oarsmen promptly took up whatever was handy and beat her to death. Agrippina saw all this and remained prudently quiet. Slipping calmly into the bay, she managed to swim to safety. There could be no doubt in her mind about Nero's treachery, but for once Agrippina did not react like a wounded tiger. The danger had at last become real, and she decided that her continued safety lay in a feigned ignorance of the plot.

Nero was waiting at his palace for good news. He learned instead that Agrippina had survived, and his immediate reaction showed how much he feared Agrippina and her wrath. "She'll come for vengeance!" Tacitus has Nero crying. "What if she arms the slaves, or rouses the soldiers? She may bring in the Senate and people, and blame me for the shipwreck, her wounds, and her friends' murder! How can I save myself?" Nero was terrified that Agrippina, who had used every means in her power to make him emperor, including murdering her own husband, would hardly stop now at toppling him. Frantic, Nero called in Burrus and Seneca for help.

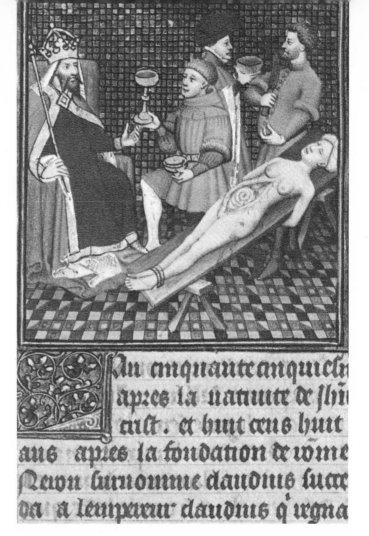

An cinquante cinquicsi
apres la nativite de jhe
suist. et huit ceus huit
aus apres la fondation de rome
Neron surnomme claudius suce
da a lempereur claudius q regna

A medieval manuscript portrays Nero presiding over Agrippina's autopsy. It is unlikely that an autopsy was performed, but the horrific nature of her death spawned many lurid tales of Nero's depravity.

Tacitus states that it was unclear whether either Burrus or Seneca had prior knowledge of the plot against Agrippina, but both men must have felt that now there was no going back. Agrippina was lethal; she had allies everywhere, and if she married a man who claimed imperial descent to any degree, there would be no stopping her. Such continuous enmity between the emperor and his mother was becoming intolerable and might eventually produce a civil war. When Seneca proposed to Burrus that the praetorian guard kill Agrippina, Burrus reminded him of the guard's loyalty to the memory of Agrippina's father, Germanicus. Burrus, not a particularly eloquent man, but one who always spoke his mind, was of the opinion that Anicetus should finish the

job he had started. Nero was overjoyed at this decision. He claimed that the first day of his reign was beginning.

When a slave sent by Agrippina arrived at Nero's palace to announce her miraculous rescue from the "accident," Nero deliberately dropped a sword at the man's feet, whereupon he was arrested and charged with plotting to murder the emperor. At the same time, Anicetus and his men stole into Agrippina's villa and killed her, beating and stabbing her to death. Pointing to the womb that bore Nero, she is said to have cried, "Strike here!"

Nero wasted no time leaving Rome for Naples, perhaps to flee from a guilty conscience, but more likely because he feared a hostile reaction to Agrippina's murder from the army or the people. He informed the Senate by letter of the arrest of the slave and of Agrippina's alleged plot against him, saying she had chosen suicide when her crime failed. Heaping on the blame, he then attacked her for all the ills of Claudius's reign.

Nero need not have worried about a negative reaction. When his letter with its lies was read aloud in the Senate, most senators vied to offer thanks for the emperor's escape from such a dangerous woman. The truth was that Agrippina had been detested, and these lawmakers were not sorry to see her out of the way, even if it took illegal methods and the emperor's henchmen to do the job. One senator, however, Publius Clodius Thrasea Paetus, walked out as the letter was being read. Thrasea was descended from one of the oldest and most noble Roman families. Like Seneca, he was a Stoic, and his courageous stand against the emperor's matricide was a stinging blow to Nero. The sycophantic reaction of the majority of the Senate, however, proved to Nero that the restraints on his actions were considerably lax. Confident that no one could harm him now, Nero added one more family murder to his list. He ordered the poisoning of Domitia Lepida, the aunt who had taken him in when his mother was exiled. He then confiscated all her property at Baiae. Nero was finally in control.

> *He tried to poison [Agrippina] three times, but she had always taken the antidote in advance; so he rigged up a machine in the ceiling of her bedroom which would dislodge the panels . . . on her while she slept. However, one of the people involved in the plot gave the secret away.*
> —SUETONIUS
> Roman historian

5

Nero's Empire

In view of Nero's desire to wield complete control over the empire, it is perhaps surprising that he did not show more interest in the provinces. During his reign, Rome was involved in a protracted war in the east, and two serious revolts occurred that required the intervention of the Roman military. Nero's main concern seems to have been that the peace was maintained in the provinces and the imperial revenues continued to flow into Rome. Fortunately for Nero, the conflicts did not require his direct intervention. The emperor was uninterested in leading soldiers; he considered himself too refined and sensitive for the roughness of warfare.

The eastern frontier of the Roman Empire had always been troublesome. When Nero came to power, Rome had just lost its control over the kingdom of Armenia, located to the south of the Caucasus Mountains. Armenia was important to the Romans because it served as a buffer state to the larger, more aggressive Parthian Empire, which stretched south and east of Armenia from the border

> The truth was Nero was not interested in governing the Empire. He never properly applied his intelligence to the task; he remained throughout his life an intuitive dilettante. This sensitivity brought him some success in diplomacy, but he had no devotion to duty of the hard business of government.
> —ALLAN MASSIE
> British historian

A Roman soldier fights a barbarian, the term used for provincial natives. During Nero's reign, three major military struggles involved the Roman army. Nero, who feared battle and abhorred military life, quickly appointed others to suppress the rebellions.

Roman soldiers interlock their shields in a protective formation. The army was composed of tough career soldiers who spent hard lives in the provinces. Nero made the crucial mistake of not cultivating the soldiers' goodwill.

of Syria, another Roman province, to what is modern Afghanistan. The Armenians appealed to Nero for aid against the Parthians, who had invaded and captured the capital city of Artaxata. The king of Parthia, Vologaeses, had installed his brother Tiridates on the Armenian throne. Nero appointed Gnaeus Domitius Corbulo to carry out the military operations.

In A.D. 55, Corbulo began preparations for the Parthian war. One problem he had to deal with was a political nuisance in the person of Quadratus, the governor of Syria, who resented the presence of the young, talented commander and wastefully duplicated his moves. The troops themselves posed an additional worry, and it took Corbulo three years to whip into shape the eastern legions that, as Tacitus puts it, "had been brought up from Syria, where they had long grown idle in peacetime service."

By the spring of A.D. 58, after a hard winter spent near Erzerum (in modern northeast Turkey) to toughen up his men, Corbulo was ready to launch the attack into Armenia and rout the Parthians. Tiridates could not count on aid from Vologaeses, who was busy with a revolt in his empire, and so was urged by Corbulo to appeal to Nero for recognition as ruler of Armenia, in effect recognizing Roman supremacy over the country. Vologaeses, however, refused to let Tiridates submit to Rome, and Corbulo continued his campaign. In the summer's fighting the Roman army captured Artaxata. During the next two years, Corbulo would capture the second major city, Tigranocerta, and report to Nero that Armenia was secure. Nero decided to seat on the Armenian throne a puppet ruler named Tigranes, who proved very unpopular.

Nero's bad judgment in selecting Tigranes ended up prolonging the conflict with Parthia. When Tigranes attacked a dependent kingdom of Parthia, King Vologaeses resolved to conquer not only Armenia but also Syria. Corbulo was now responsible for Syria; his antagonistic colleague Quadratus had died. He informed Nero that Syria, an important imperial province, was in danger. Corbulo threat-

ened to invade Mesopotamia (part of Parthia), and Vologaeses, aware of the Roman commander's abilities, came to an agreement. Nero promptly abandoned Tigranes and sent a Roman official to rule Armenia directly. Unfortunately, this latest appointment proved Nero's judgment had not improved; Lucius Caesennius Paetus nearly destroyed the Roman presence in the area through his military incompetence. The war with Parthia would drag on, draining Roman finances and manpower in the east, until A.D. 66.

In A.D. 61 the Roman army in Britain faced a widespread rebellion. Britain had come under Roman control during the reign of Claudius; its conquest had been relatively easy — within four years of the Roman invasion in A.D. 43, the south had submitted — but there remained pockets of opposition, and the Romans had continued to expand north and west to consolidate their rule. In A.D. 61 Suetonius Paulinus, commander in Britain, heard of the revolt of the Iceni tribe and its allies. The exact reasons for the rebellion remain unclear. Tacitus lays the blame squarely on the Romans' treatment of the native

In A.D. 61 Queen Boudicca led the Iceni tribe of Britain in a rebellion against the Romans. The revolt was put down, but it succeeded in stopping the expansion of the Romans into the north and west of the island.

Britons, describing that upon the death of Prasutagus, a client king (one who acknowledged the overlordship of Rome), the Roman army ravaged his kingdom, flogging Boudicca, his widow, and driving the British nobles from their land. It has also been reported that the expenses for maintaining the Roman presence in Britain — including financing fortresses, roads, and providing for the army — were impoverishing the local tribes. Dio Cassius, a 2nd-century A.D. Roman historian and politician, depicts Boudicca as a fiery Celtic warrior, tall and red-headed, fiercely urging the Britons on. The revolt encompassed East Anglia on the coast northeast of London and spread west and north to the Midlands. The Britons first attacked unwalled Camulodunum (Colchester) and burned it. Suetonius retreated to London but decided that it could not be held because it too was unwalled. The Britons then destroyed London and Verulamium (St. Albans). Tacitus states that 70,000 Romans and their allies were killed by the rampaging Britons. Finally, at a battle whose site is unclear, perhaps in Essex, Suetonius defeated the Britons. On the battlefield the superior training of the Roman soldiers overwhelmed the tribal warriors, and many thousands of them perished. Boudicca, determined to escape capture, committed suicide.

Roman soldiers erect a trophy beside their barbarian prisoners. Romans often respected the physical courage and ferocious spirit of the provincial tribes and celebrated their victories with traditional military parades known as triumphs.

Nero sent one of his advisers, the freedman Polyclitus, to report on the situation in Britain. The vanquished Britons jeered Polyclitus but did not resume the rebellion, and Britain was calm for the remainder of Nero's reign. The Romans, however, deciding that they had reached their limit on this faraway island, gave up their plans to conquer Wales in the west.

Events at Rome in the early 60s A.D. showed that Nero was becoming more absolute in his rule and increasingly unwilling to defer to the advice or judgment of the Senate or Seneca. Despite the early promise of cooperation, the relationship between Nero and the Senate was deteriorating. Nero's last gesture of deference to the Senate came in A.D. 61, when he upheld the death penalty decreed by the Senate against an entire household of slaves. The slaves were condemned because one had killed their master, Lucius Pedanius Secundus, the prefect of Rome. The Roman nobles were genuinely frightened about slave uprisings and tended to deal harshly with slaves who broke the law. Roman law decreed that if a slave killed his or her master, all slaves in the household were to be executed. Pedanius had several hundred household slaves.

Despite their generally bloodthirsty temperament, the Roman plebs occasionally displayed a sentimental side. They now rose up in revulsion against the proposed execution of 400 slaves for the crime of only one man. Partly this had to do with the spectacle of sending innocent women and children to their deaths, but also the people had a thorough dislike of the aristocratic Senate and enjoyed thwarting its desires. While the Senate debated the issue, the mob thronged the streets outside the Senate house. The Senate passed the death penalty, while the mob, armed with torches and stones, lined the route the slaves were to follow in order to prevent the execution.

Nero did not like to sign such execution orders. In addition, most of his chief ministers were former slaves who probably encouraged his sympathy. Yet Nero accepted the Senate's decision and called out

A statuette of a slave boy who has fallen asleep waiting for his master. Nero's last gesture of conciliation to the Senate involved upholding a death verdict against an entire household of slaves because one had killed the master.

Slaves rebel against their masters. In Nero's time, the Romans greatly feared slave revolts, and the penalties for slaves who committed crimes were extremely harsh.

the soldiers to suppress the discontented plebs. All the slaves were put to death.

The following year, A.D. 62, was a turning point in Nero's reign. When Burrus, the praetorian commander, died that year, Nero seems to have thrown off the restraints he had felt in the presence of his early advisers. Seneca came under blistering attack from men seeking favor with Nero, and perhaps seeing a change for the worse in his relationship with the emperor, Seneca wisely retired from public life. The two men who had run the imperial government in good conscience were both gone.

Nero appointed two men to replace Burrus as commander of the praetorian guard: Faenius Rufus, and the hateful Gaius Ofonius Tigellinus, one of the more sinister and depraved figures of Nero's later reign. Tacitus says of Tigellinus that "Nero found his unending immoralities and evil reputation fascinating."

With the appointment of Tigellinus, Nero's descent into tyranny was firmly set. As in the case of Poppaea, who was growing impatient with the role of mistress, Tigellinus's social standing was not terribly high, and he too appealed to Nero's worst instincts. Such were the people now advising the emperor, and their efforts were not intended to serve the best interests of the empire but to maintain their own positions of influence. They alternately flattered Nero or manipulated his weaknesses. Tigellinus went to work at once. He revived Nero's fear of rivals, poisoning him against Rubellius Plautus,

who now lived in exile in the province of Asia (modern western Turkey). Tigellinus stressed Plautus's imperial origins and his closeness to an imperial army in the east. Nero sent soldiers for Plautus, who was killed and beheaded. Tigellinus also prejudiced Nero against one Cornelius Sulla, whom the emperor ordered murdered at his home in Marseilles, in southern France. Sulla was completely unaware of the charges of conspiracy against him. In this way Tigellinus ingratiated himself with the emperor, who felt that the praetorian commander's actions against potential enemies proved his loyalty and devotion.

With Agrippina, Burrus, and Seneca out of his way and with the backing of servile senators who, with the exception of the implacable Thrasea Plautus, would fall over themselves to stay in his good graces, Nero took his next bold step. He divorced Octavia on the grounds of barrenness and married Poppaea, who was now pregnant.

Nero may have thought he no longer had to support his claim to the throne by his relationship with Claudius, but he expected some opposition to his divorce from the daughter of a former emperor. What he did not anticipate was the fierce reaction of the Roman plebs, who championed Octavia to the point where Nero was forced to send soldiers to contain them. Poppaea, perhaps fearing for her own safety, now stoked Nero's fears of being overthrown. She hinted that Octavia could easily find a husband with royal blood who would pose a serious threat to Nero.

Nero again resorted to theater of a sinister and tragic sort. Anicetus was brought on stage once more, with the promise of a large reward and the threat of execution if he refused. He made a perjurious confession of adultery with Octavia and was banished to the island of Sardinia to live out the remainder of his life in peaceful oblivion. Octavia was charged with treason and attempted revolution and was exiled to Pandateria. She was executed in June A.D. 62. Twelve days later Nero married the widely detested Poppaea.

The cruelty of Octavia's humiliating death showed that Nero was beginning to lose all control of his fears and suspicions.
—MICHAEL GRANT
British historian

6

The Great Fire

As Seneca had understood, the strongest restraint on Nero had been his domineering mother. With Agrippina out of the way, Nero was free to range in directions that appealed to his emotions and were intended solely for his own personal gratification. He started racing chariots, which had aroused his mother's scorn. To lessen the spectacle of the emperor driving a four-horse chariot, Seneca and Burrus had prevailed on Nero to indulge his passion at a private racecourse built outside the city. Even in this private setting, word of the emperor's actions got out, and an audience gathered that was composed primarily, according to Suetonius, of "slaves and loungers."

As Nero pursued his dreams of artistic fame, his political hand became heavier and his judgments more arbitrary. No matter how great the adulation from adoring audiences and fawning senators, it was never enough to still all of Nero's insecurities.

While the city was burning, it was rumored that Nero had been so moved by the sight that he took his lyre, put on his singer's robes and sang through the whole of a tragic song . . . when [the population] heard [this] story, [they] could very easily jump to the conclusion that, if he found the fire so exciting, he must have started it.
—MICHAEL GRANT
British historian

A painting from the catacombs of Rome depicts a Christian woman. After the Great Fire of Rome, Nero made the tiny sect the scapegoat for his own troubles, and in Christian literature Nero is portrayed as a relentless persecutor.

Freed from the restraining influences of his mother and Seneca, who retired in A.D. 62, Nero indulged in his passion for chariot racing. The emperor's delight in personally driving the chariot, led normally by slaves or commoners, shocked respectable Roman families.

In A.D. 61 Nero reinstituted treason trials as the quickest way to rid himself of opponents and seize their property, as well. As soon as Tigellinus whispered the possibility of revolt, another rival was dispatched. Nero began the fateful year of A.D. 64 with the persecution of the final Silanus brother, Torquatus, whose only real crime, according to Tacitus, was his descent from Augustus. Torquatus was denounced for extravagant generosity, the purpose of which — according to Nero — could only be imperial ambition. Torquatus chose to open his veins rather than wait for the Senate to pass the expected death sentence.

Nero had traveled to Beneventum on the east coast in preparation for a trip to Greece, but he suddenly canceled his plans and returned to Rome. He celebrated his intention to stay in Rome with a lavish, scandalous spectacle given by Tigellinus in which, according to Tacitus, the emperor "tried every pleasure, licensed and unlicensed." The events of that summer would prove just how unpopular the young emperor had become for his debauched life-style.

On the night of July 18, a fire broke out in one end of the *Circus Maximus*, the huge, open, oval-shaped arena (*circus* means circle or oval) that held chariot races and triumphal processions, located in the valley between the Palatine and Aventine hills. A strong wind blew the flames to the nearby shops, which contained inflammable material, and within a very short time the fire was raging out of control. There is a description of the resulting horror and panic by Tacitus: "All movement was blocked by the terrified, shrieking women, by helpless old people or children, by those who sought their own safety or tried to help others. . . . When they looked back, outbreaks of fire threatened them from the front or the rear. When they reached a neighboring quarter, that too was alight: even what they had supposed to be remote districts were found to be affected."

Rome was divided into 14 administrative districts. The Great Fire demolished three of them, and only four remained untouched by the flames. The other seven were damaged to varying degrees. The Forum, the commercial and administrative center of the city, and the Capitoline hill, the religious center on which stood the important temple of Jupiter Capitolinus, escaped destruction, as did part of the Palatine hill, the site of the most luxurious homes.

The Circus Maximus was an enormous oval arena designed for chariot racing and triumphal parades. Prominent political figures and emperors paid for public shows to solicit favor from the attending plebs.

A dramatic portrayal of Nero shows him playing the lyre while Rome is engulfed by flames. According to Roman historian Suetonius, Nero greeted the news of the blaze with the recitation of a tragic poem.

But many of the densely packed tenement buildings, several temples from republican Rome, public buildings, Vesta's shrine to Rome's household gods (the *lares* and *penates*), masterpieces of art from Greece, and innumerable records of Roman life were all lost to the fire. After the fire had been burning for six days, a row of houses at the foot of the Esquiline hill was demolished in an attempt to create a firebreak to halt the blaze, but the fire could not be contained and continued for three more days.

Nero was approximately 30 miles south of Rome at the coastal town of Antium (modern Anzio) when the fire broke out. However, he did not return to the capital until his own palace — the *Domus Transitoria* — was threatened. The structure was, indeed, completely destroyed. Upon his arrival in Rome, Nero instituted several immediate measures for the relief of the homeless. He had temporary housing erected in the Campus Martius, the huge field located to the north of the city that was used for military exercises and some political meetings. To provide additional places for those whose homes had been destroyed, Nero opened up his own gardens and some of the large public buildings. He ordered more food brought into Rome from the port of Ostia and neighboring towns, and he lowered the price of grain.

In the aftermath of the fire, Nero eagerly turned to the task of reconstructing the devastated parts of the city. He offered bonuses for clearing the rubble and rebuilding. Where possible, he laid out the city along clear lines to avoid the narrow, rambling streets crowded by blocks of tenements. He even issued some farsighted ordinances that regulated tenement height (people lived as high as the sixth story in these dark, overcrowded buildings) and street widths. He ordered that each building have separating walls and each household its own fire-fighting equipment. The new building plans provided for open spaces along the streets to prevent the tenement fronts from standing right at the street edges. The emperor also extended the water supply in the city. Nero was praised by Tacitus for the sensible building plan, which "added to the beauty of the new city."

Apartment buildings, such as this structure in Pompeii, burned like tinder in the Great Fire of Rome. Densely packed together and filled with debris, the buildings burned quickly, helping to spread the flames through the city.

Rome's water supply was dependent on a system of aqueducts such as this one well outside the city. The water lines, however, were of little help in controlling the fire. After the blaze, Nero extended the water supply in Rome to those left homeless.

The fact that Nero's generous and decisive actions to help the Romans recoup and rebuild could not stop certain squalid rumors concerning his behavior during the fire was proof of how much he had alienated the Romans, including the plebs. At the height of the blaze, word had spread that it had been deliberately set, and all the ancient sources report that Nero was held responsible. Only Tacitus brings up the possibility that the fire was accidental. Suetonius and Dio Cassius recount the story that Nero, upon seeing Rome in flames, recited an original poem on the fall of Troy. Modern scholars generally reject the idea that Nero set the fire. At the time, however, the rumor proved hard to dispel. According to Tacitus, there were reports that attempts to put out the fire had been stopped by roving bands of thugs who, it was believed, must have been in the employ of the emperor.

Nero proceeded to undo all the good work he had started by erecting a new palace for himself, the enormous *Domus Aurea*—the Golden House—right in the middle of what had been the most densely populated part of the city. Not since Nero has a mon-

arch appropriated so much of a city — more than 300 acres in the heart of Rome — for his own purposes. As planned by Nero, the Domus Aurea was a spectacle even the pleasure-loving Romans found hard to believe. Suetonius gives a vivid description of the extraordinarily luxurious and splendid palace: "The entrance hall was large enough to contain a huge statue of himself, 120 feet high; and the pillared arcade ran for a whole mile. An enormous pool, like a sea, was surrounded by buildings made to resemble cities, and by a landscape garden consisting of ploughed fields, vineyards, pastures, and woodlands — where every variety of domestic and wild animal roamed about. Parts of the house were overlaid with gold and studded with precious stones and mother-of-pearl. All the dining rooms had ceilings of fretted ivory, the panels of which could slide back and let a rain of flowers, or of perfume from hidden sprinklers, shower upon his guests. The main dining room was circular, and its roof revolved, day and night, in time with the sky. Sea water, or sulphur water, was always on tap in the baths." Nero is reported to have said in delight that he could finally "live like a human being."

This interior view shows the elegance and sophistication of the homes owned by the wealthy. The Palatine, the richest section of Rome, was one of the few areas spared in the Great Fire.

The grandiose scale of Nero's dream house showed how much he was losing touch with the reality of his position in Rome. The Domus Aurea was exceedingly unpopular with the people — who were now crowded into an even smaller area within the city — and with the upper classes, who resented the emperor's wasteful spending of imperial monies on such a grossly inappropriate project. The poet Martial (Marcus Valerius Martialis), the master of the epigram (a concise, often satirical short poem or saying), wrote of the Domus Aurea:

Here where the heavenly colossus has a close
view of the stars
And high structures rise on the lofty road,
There once shone the hated hall of the cruel
king
And one house took up the whole of Rome.

So it must have felt to the people whose property had been expropriated to make way for Nero's grand folly. In fact, the Domus Aurea was never completed; some 10 years later Emperor Vespasian (Titus Flavius Sabinus Vespasianus) converted most of the

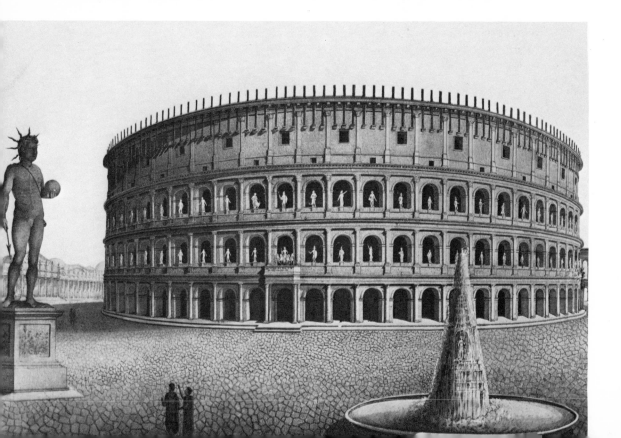

A reconstruction of the original appearance of the Roman Colosseum. The huge arena was not constructed until after Nero's death, when his opulent, unfinished Golden House was torn down to make room for it.

St. Paul brought the word of Christ to the Gentiles and was vital in the spread of Christianity to the cities of the Roman Empire. Christian tradition holds that Paul perished in the persecution conducted by Nero, but his actual fate is unknown.

palace and its gardens into public property. On the site he began construction of the Colosseum, the huge amphitheater that may have been so named after the colossal bronze statue of Nero. The ruins of the Colosseum still stand in Rome.

The fire had conveniently destroyed a huge area where Nero now was building his Golden House. The emperor found himself faced with a hostile city mob that remained convinced he had started the blaze to acquire the land for his palace. As normally happened with all natural disasters, a wave of superstitious panic had consumed the Romans after the fire. The priests consulted the prophetic Sibylline books, looking for a way to appease the gods, but Tacitus states that "no human aid, no largesse from the emperor, no supplications to heaven, did anything to ease the impression that the fire had been deliberately started. Nero looked around for a scapegoat, and inflicted the most fiendish tortures on a group of persons already hated by the people for their crimes. This was the sect known as Christians."

A monument shows crucified Christian martyrs. Nero, blamed by many Romans for the fire, persecuted the Christians as scapegoats. The cult of saints began when Christians made heroes of those who were tortured and executed and built shrines on the sites of their deaths.

This crucial passage in Tacitus is the first mention by a pagan author of the Christians. Nero's reasons for blaming this tiny group for the Great Fire remain obscure. Indeed, Tacitus is the only ancient author to state specifically that the Christians were Nero's scapegoats, so the entire issue is problematic. However, within the Christian tradition, Nero is a persecutor, so it seems likely that Tacitus is correct. The Christians, conveniently for the emperor, did believe that the world would soon be destroyed by fire. Nero likely saw that the Christians would have no defenders in Rome — they were poor (many were slaves), unpopular, and misunderstood — and so made the perfect scapegoat for his own troubles.

The Christians were the followers of the teachings of Jesus Christ, a Jewish preacher in the Roman province of Judaea (modern Israel) who declared that the kingdom of God had arrived on earth in his person. Christ had gained a strong, widespread popularity among the native poor people of the region, but he came into conflict with the established

Jewish political leaders, the Sadducees, in Jerusalem. He was turned over to the Roman authorities, and Pontius Pilate, the prefect, or governor, of Judaea, had him tried as a subversive. Christ's treasonable crime in the eyes of Rome was that he did not deny being the king of the Jews, a direct challenge to the imperial authority. Christ was crucified, a common means of execution, but his disciples spread his teachings throughout the eastern provinces. Saul, a Jew from the Greek city of Tarsus in Asia Minor, adopted the Christian beliefs and traveled widely through the empire preaching the word of Christ. During the 40s and 50s, St. Paul, as he is known, was instrumental in bringing the teachings of the rather obscure Judaean holy man to the Gentiles, or non-Jews. Word of his lectures spread through the major cities of the empire, and finally, the faith professed by the followers of Jesus Christ reached the capital, Rome.

Under Nero, the Christians were not subject to official state persecution, as they would be under later emperors. Foreign cults were not forbidden in Rome; some were even popular, as long as formal obeisance to the emperor was enforced. Eastern cults were tolerated until they threatened to create public unrest. The cults of Isis, from Egypt, and Bacchus, from Greece, had been banned under Tiberius because the wild nature of their celebrations bred public disorder. The Christian cult, however, was different from the other Eastern religions popular in Rome, because it was an exclusive religion — the Christians worshiped only one god. The Christian rituals, especially the Eucharist, were misunderstood by the Romans, who heard only that these strange people were eating the body and drinking the blood of their god. To the Romans, the mysterious and secret rites were scandalous, and the denial of the Roman pantheon of gods bordered on treason.

Nero thus faced no opposition to his roundup of the Christians in Rome. Many of the unfortunate believers were burned alive, a standard Roman punishment for arson. Nero also had them sent into the amphitheater to be used as entertainment for the

masses. Tacitus writes that "dressed in the skins of wild animals [the Christians] were torn to pieces by dogs, or crucified or burned alive, being used as torches when daylight ended. . . ." The brutality of Nero's acts against the Christians was so great that the Romans, despite their dislike for the sect, felt sorry for them because they were being executed only to serve Nero's own ends. In his palace gardens and in the Circus, Nero, often dressed as a chari-

A caricature of gluttony was easily recognizable to Roman theatergoers. Among Nero's excesses was a gargantuan appetite, and later portraits of the emperor show him as grotesquely corpulent.

The Magna Mater (Great Mother) was a goddess imported to Rome from Carthage, North Africa. Most foreign cults, including Christianity, were legal under Nero. Later emperors would make persecution of the Christians an official imperial policy.

oteer, presided over the gruesome spectacle of the persecution of the Christians.

Nero had by this time ruled for 10 years. It was a sign of the power he now wielded that people thought him powerful enough — and degraded enough — to start the fire that devoured his own city. Nero's depravities, encouraged by Tigellinus, descended to new lows. Suetonius relates an episode that may or may not be true but that is consistent with the picture of a man becoming mad with the possibilities of his own power: At a party in his gardens, Nero, dressed in the skins of a wild animal, attacked the genitals of men and women bound to stakes. Nero lived only for his own gratification. He wanted to be larger than life, and his ambitions led him to a place the Romans considered unfit for an emperor—the stage.

7

The Artist Emerges

Since the days of his youth, Nero had always shown a keen interest in the arts and a passion for horses. As emperor, he was in a position to indulge his dreams for artistic accomplishment and to afford any entertainment he desired. His chief loves became singing to his own lyre accompaniment and chariot racing. Suetonius reports that not long after Nero became emperor, he invited the great lyre player Terpnus to give him lessons. He followed a rigorous schedule of practice and discipline to develop his voice. For hours he lay on his back with a lead weight on his chest to develop his chest muscles. He resorted to enemas and purgatives to control his weight and avoided food like apples and tomatoes that were said to be bad for the voice. In the end, he developed a creditable, husky voice.

Every artist wants an audience, and Nero was no exception. He craved mass recognition and applause, but in the early years of his reign he was aware of the shock a public stage appearance by the emperor would create in Rome, so he started slowly, on a smaller scale. He tried his voice out before a selected audience in A.D. 59, in his private gardens.

[Nero] was the first ruler in all recorded history, and indeed almost the only one of any real importance, to consider himself primarily as a singer and stage performer.
—MICHAEL GRANT
British historian

In Greek mythology, Orpheus played the lyre so beautifully that he charmed wild beasts and birds. After the Great Fire, Nero devoted his time to reciting, playing the lyre, and singing on stage. He was as disciplined in improving his voice as he was irresponsible in conducting state business.

A Roman bas-relief portrays a comic scene from the theater. When performing on stage, Nero not only dictated the plays to be shown and the actors to appear, he also filled his audiences with paid admirers, the *Augustiani*.

For the occasion he established a festival called the *Juvenalia* — the Youth Games — to celebrate the Roman tradition commemorating the first shaving of a young man's beard. (Nero was 22 at the time.) Dramatic and musical performances were held, and it is recorded that members of the senatorial and equestrian classes — most likely those who wanted to stay in Nero's good graces — participated. A show accompanied Nero's ritual shaving, and his shorn beard was placed in a pearl-and-gold box and dedicated at the temple of Jupiter. The highlight of the festival came with the appearance of the emperor on stage, performing tragic arias on his lyre. As insurance, Nero had brought together a group of young men, called the *Augustiani*, as a kind of accompanying fan club for the emperor's performances; they led the vociferous applause. Tacitus writes in disgust that the Augustiani "kept the applause going day and night and bestowed on Nero's beauty of person and voice epithets reserved for the gods." According to Suetonius, the equestrian leaders of the Augustiani were amply rewarded with gold for each performance.

Nero surrounded himself with artists and established a kind of amateur literary club, at which he and his friends would compose poetry. They held lavish banquets that lasted from noon until midnight, gorging on such dishes as peacock tongue flavored with cinnamon and yellow pig à la Trojan. (When the pig was carved, hot sausages fell out and live thrushes escaped.) Among Nero's literary friends was Lucan (Marcus Annaeus Lucanus), Seneca's nephew, whose reputation as a poet was rapidly growing. Suetonius and Tacitus disagree on Nero's own poetic talents. Suetonius says he never borrowed from others and composed verses "enthusiastically, without any effort." Tacitus criticizes Nero's poetry, only a few lines of which have survived, for lacking "vigour, inspiration and uniformity of style." Nero's best-known literary work was the *Troica*, a retelling of the fall of Troy, in which he changed the traditional ending. On the whole, it appears that Nero's literary talents, like his singing, were on the mediocre side, but not entirely bad.

This fresco depiction of a poetry reading comes from Pompeii. Nero formed an amateur literary club and gave poetry recitations at lavish banquets. His vanity, however, would not allow him to admit real talent in others, and he set out to destroy any artistic competitors.

A classical Greek vase shows athletes practicing. Nero based his Neronia, an athletic and artistic competition, on the Olympic Games of Greece.

In A.D. 60 Nero introduced in Rome a new competition modeled on the Greek Olympic contests. First called the *certamen quinquennale* (the contest of every fifth year), the spectacle, which lasted for several days, came to be known as the Neronia. It consisted of three sections: music (which included poetry and rhetoric); athletics and gymnastics; and chariot racing. Nero faced a good deal of opposition from upper-class Romans, who had little respect for organized athletics, which were associated in their minds with the Greeks, but Nero drew the judges of the contests from men of upper-class consular rank and encouraged the Roman nobility to take part in the music contests. At the first Neronia the emperor did not participate, but he made it clear that it was only a matter of time before he would.

In public the official Roman was a dignified individual, displaying the traditional virtue of *gravitas* — a seriousness of thought and purpose and a reserved manner. This behavior was reflected in the Roman national dress — the toga — which, when properly worn, was impressive and graceful. Below the toga was worn a tunic: a shirt with short sleeves that reached to the knees and was girded by a belt. Both of these were customarily white. Nero offended imperial dignity by receiving audiences in a garment that was a mix between a toga and a tunic, brilliantly colored and set off at the neck by a colorful scarf. Equally unorthodox was his choice of a multicolored tunic topped with a frilly muslin collar. He took to arranging his blond hair in rows of curls —

"in steps," according to Suetonius — a style modeled on that of actors and charioteers.

Nero was also extravagant. In addition to his private wealth, the emperor could enjoy the immense riches of the empire, and he increasingly made little distinction between the two. Nero never wore the same garment twice. He paid the huge sum of 4 million *sesterces* (a standard Roman currency) for embroidered Babylonian sofa covers. He gave a grand estate to his favorite gladiator, Spiculus, and another to a lyre player named Menecrates for singing beautiful songs. Normally, such valuable property was a reward for special service to the state. Nero, it was felt, was cheapening traditional Roman political values.

Nero, who thirsted for popularity, was a master showman. In addition to the innumerable plays he put on at the theater and gladiator shows, his games at the Circus were so lavish and offered so many prizes that the public was no longer satisfied with those given by ordinary magistrates. This extravagance endeared him to the ordinary Roman, and his appearances at the games prompted the tremendous popular enthusiasm he adored.

A mural from a Pompeii house portrays waterfront villas owned by the wealthy in the countryside. Upper-class Romans were strict traditionalists and were grossly offended by Nero's flamboyant behavior.

In A.D. 64 Nero decided to take the plunge and perform on a public stage. Still afraid that to do so in Rome would generate too much opposition, the emperor traveled south to Naples, which had originally been founded as a Greek colony and thus enjoyed a more liberal tradition in artistic matters than did Rome. Nero trod the boards playing the lyre and singing Greek tragedies. The very idea of an emperor before the footlights undoubtedly titillated the locals, who crowded in to see the performance.

In case there was any lag in enthusiasm, Nero had brought his traveling fan club, the Augustiani, which was divided into three sections. The first section, called the Bees, kept up a humming din, the Roof Tiles clapped with hollowed hands, and the third group, nicknamed the Bricks, cheered with flat-handed claps. Nero was thrilled that his first appearance was such a phenomenal success and immediately made plans for a trip to Greece, where, he felt, the stodgy Romans would learn how a true artist was appreciated. After setting out for the west coast of Italy, however, Nero suddenly changed his mind and turned back for Rome.

A model of the Roman theater of Marcellinus. In A.D. 64 Nero traveled to Naples to hold his first stage performance. He feared appearing in Rome because of the scandal his public recital would cause.

It is generally accepted that Nero did not have any inkling of the plans being laid in Rome, and by early A.D. 65 the emperor would be the focus of a conspiracy against his life that would reveal a widespread discontent with his rule and provoke a crisis with the senatorial class. The plot centered around, although it did not originate with, Gaius Calpurnius Piso, a nobleman from an old republican family. Exiled by Caligula, who had stolen his wife, Piso was recalled by Claudius and served in some respectable government posts. Popular with the people for his friendliness and generosity, he was a literary patron and an amateur poet. He was not the ideal man, however, around whom to build a conspiracy, because he preferred talk to action. He would make a fatal delay when confronted with the need for a decision.

The common bond among the conspirators was probably not as much a desire to see any one man, including Piso, in power as it was a wish to be rid of Nero. They made up a loosely knit group of different social classes, including senators, equestrians, soldiers, and even a former slave. Tacitus names as two of the most active participants Subrius Flavus, tribune of the praetorians, and Sulpicius Asper, a centurion, or army officer. Lucan, Nero's former fellow poet, who had fallen from favor when the emperor became jealous of his literary work, was among the plotters. Lucan was probably angry that he had been forbidden to publish by Nero, but he may have joined ultimately because of strong Stoic and republican beliefs. Plautius Later-

A procession of priests and senators, the bastions of Roman traditional virtues, is detailed on a monument built by Augustus. Nero violated the codes of Roman public behavior, even modifying the dignified toga with brightly colored scarves and tunics.

anus, who came from one of Rome's wealthiest families, joined out of patriotic motives and love for Rome; Flavius Scaevinus and Afranius Quintianus, who became involved in the plot at an early stage, were both senators who felt they had suffered insults at the hands of Nero.

The initial core of conspirators began to draw in members of the equestrian class; of these Tacitus mentions Claudius Senecio, a former friend of Nero, and Antonius Natalis, a close friend of Piso's. Several members of Rome's main equestrian business families joined. One of the most important to add his name to the conspirators was Faenius Rufus, the cocommander of the praetorian guard, who feared that his position with the emperor was being undermined by Tigellinus. The conspirators knew that for any rebellion to succeed in Rome the participation, or at least the tacit support, of the praetorian guard was crucial, so Faenius's defection was greeted with optimism.

Perhaps the strangest member of the entire group was the freedwoman Epicharis. Little is known of her background, but as the plot unraveled she exhibited more courage than most of the men involved. The plot to assassinate Nero came to a head in April A.D. 65. Tired of the delays and indecision on the part of the main conspirators as to when and how to kill Nero, Epicharis traveled to Misenum, where she apparently tried to get the prefect of the fleet to join the conspirators. Nero often went sailing — how ironic it would be if he were to perish at sea, as he had planned for Agrippina! When the fleet captain brought Epicharis's discussion to the attention of the emperor, Epicharis, who had cunningly avoided giving out names or details, denied the charge. Because there were no witnesses, Epicharis could not be condemned, but Nero had her held while an investigation began into a possible conspiracy.

Unaware that Epicharis had told Nero nothing, the conspirators hurried to carry out their plans before the entire plot was revealed. After rejecting several plans, they decided to kill Nero in Rome while

he was attending games at the Circus. Piso was to wait nearby, and when Nero was dead, Piso would be taken to the praetorian camp to be proclaimed emperor. On the night before the planned assassination, however, the behavior of Senator Scaevinus aroused the suspicions of one of his servants, Milichus, who went to the emperor. Scaevinus was arrested, and although he ably excused his unusual actions, the downfall of the conspirators was ensured when the freedman brought up the name of Natalis, who had visited with Scaevinus for several hours that night. Scaevinus and Natalis were questioned separately, and when their accounts did not match, their fates were sealed, and under the threat of torture they began revealing the names of the other conspirators.

The plot quickly came undone as men tried to save themselves by informing on as many people as possible. Scaevinus named Lucan, Quintianus, and Senecio; Natalis denounced his own friend Piso and even implicated Seneca, now long retired, whose role in the conspiracy is obscure. Lucan implicated his own mother; Senecio named his friend Annius Pollio. Epicharis, who owed no loyalty to anyone, endured a daylong torture without revealing any names or information. She committed suicide the following day before enduring any more interrogation. Tacitus writes of her: "How much nobler this example than that of freeborn men, Roman knights [equestrians] and senators, who did not even wait for the torture to betray their nearest and dearest!"

Nero, alarmed at the extent of the plot, increased his bodyguard and dispatched troops after the remaining suspects. Piso was urged to appeal to the soldiers and the people to rise up against the emperor, but he wasted precious time trying to decide what to do, and finally he committed suicide. Plautius Lateranus was killed by a tribune who had known of the plot but was trying to save his own skin. A praetorian officer was sent to inform Seneca, who was at a villa in the suburbs of Rome, of the charge of treason against him. Seneca boldly refuted the charge, but Nero was determined to be rid of his

> *At such a court it is a miracle to reach old age, and the feat can only be accomplished by accepting insult and injury with a smiling face.*
> —SENECA
> Roman statesman,
> on the state of Nero's court

Seneca calms his followers before his death. Although Seneca played no part in the Pisonian Conspiracy of A.D. **65, Nero was determined to be rid of his conscientious former adviser, who chose to die in the traditionally honorable Roman way — by committing suicide.**

old tutor, who was a reproach to the emperor's degraded way of life, and Seneca was ordered to commit suicide, which he did with dignity. Faenius Rufus, who had so far remained unnamed as a conspirator, was finally denounced and executed. Many on the periphery of the plot, or those whom Nero just wanted to be rid of, were exiled.

Nero was shaken by the conspiracy. It had involved some of the most powerful members of the Senate, the richest men in Rome; men who had once been friends, soldiers who had formerly been loyal. Afraid of further unrest among the army, Nero gave out large donatives — special gifts of money — to the soldiers to win their favor. Faenius was replaced as praetorian commander by Nymphidius Sabinus, a notoriously depraved man who claimed to be the illegitimate son of Emperor Caligula. The Senate, afraid of Nero's wrath, roundly condemned the conspirators and their sympathizers and passed several votes intended to flatter the emperor, including one to rename the month of April after him.

That same year Nero's wife died. Nero reportedly kicked the pregnant Poppaea in a fit of anger. He was filled with remorse and had Poppaea deified, as he had done with their deceased daughter Claudia. The following year Nero tried to marry Antonia, the surviving daughter of Claudius. When she refused, he had her executed on a charge of conspiracy. In

A.D. 66 Nero married Statilia Messalina, a beautiful and intelligent woman from a rich, powerful family. Nero was her fifth husband.

The emperor seemed satisfied that his enemies were dispersed, and in A.D. 65 the second Neronia took place. This time Nero decided to participate despite the Senate's attempt to bribe him not to appear on stage by awarding him beforehand the prizes for poetry and rhetoric. Nero insisted that he did not want any special treatment and would compete with the other artists; he was convinced that his talent alone would earn him accolade. Nero may even have been vain enough to believe that the judges awarded him all the first prizes because of his artistic superiority.

Nero's public performance at the Neronia was very popular with the Roman plebs. Tacitus reports, however, that visitors to the city from the more conservative, traditional Italian countryside "found the spectacle intolerable." Imperial spies reported on those whose applause was weak or those who fell asleep during Nero's performances. Tacitus writes that even the future emperor Vespasian, who was discovered nodding off during one of Nero's recitals, found it a difficult task to extricate himself from the disfavor he incurred.

This second Neronia was celebrated with particular extravagance by Nero because he was awaiting delivery of a vast amount of gold treasure from North Africa. Nero's treasure hunt in Carthage was one of his more ludicrous actions. Caesellius Bassus, an equestrian from Carthage (an ancient city near modern Tunis, Tunisia), told Nero of a dream he had that revealed the location of a cave filled with the gold treasure of Queen Dido of Carthage. (In Roman legend, Dido was the founder of Carthage and the lover of Aeneas, the legendary founder of Rome.) Without obtaining any proof of the tale, Nero dispatched ships and men to retrieve the gold. Bassus carried out extensive excavations, but of course nothing was ever found. Meanwhile, Nero was throwing away the empire's money on lavish games and entertainments.

> *He recited his own poems . . . which so delighted everyone that a Thanksgiving was voted him, as though he had won a great victory, and the passages he had chosen were printed in letters of gold on plaques dedicated to Capitoline Jupiter.*
> —SUETONIUS
> Roman historian,
> on Nero's artistic ability

MVNIFICENTIA
SS·D·N·BENEDICTI

PP· XIV

8
Tyranny

By now, the constant surfeit of riches and pleasure were taken for granted by Nero. He boasted openly that no previous emperor had ever realized the height of power he enjoyed. Indeed, nothing in the great Roman Empire was immune from the emperor's reach. Nero's "unreasonable craving for immortal fame," as Suetonius put it, even led him along the path Caligula had begun to follow: divinity.

Roman religion was polytheistic: Many gods were worshiped, and the worship took many forms. At first it did not seem unnatural to include the Roman emperor in prayers for a good life or the well-being of the empire, and from there it was only a short step to making the emperor himself into a god. The first emperor, Augustus, and his successor, Tiberius, had both tried to keep imperial worship to a minimum by putting limits on the religious honors bestowed on the emperor. Augustus was deified — made a god in the official Roman pantheon — after his death. Caligula had considered himself a living god and forced his subjects to address him as such.

> *History proves that by practicing cruelty you earn nothing but hatred.*
> —JULIUS CAESAR
> 1st-century B.C. Roman emperor

Nero's gluttony and vanity are evident in this portrait. His small features are almost lost in the bloated head and neck. The emperor wears a beard, and his long hair is elaborately curled in the style of the Greeks he so admired.

The deified emperor Augustus sits at the side of the goddess Roma. In the latter part of his reign, Nero began to adopt the symbols of divinity, behavior that reminded the suspicious Romans of the mad Caligula.

Emperor Claudius, more temperate by nature, had only to look at the backlash created by Caligula's excesses to see that he had carried the imperial cult too far. Claudius, who was deified by Nero after his death, again put restrictions on the worship of the emperor.

By Nero's time the imperial cult consisted of giving official honors to the dead, deified emperors, as well as to the living emperor. In addition, however, and especially in the eastern part of the empire, there were certain unofficial honors bestowed that approached actual worship. In many countries in the east, especially in Egypt and much of the Greek world, rulers had been looked upon as gods. In Alexandria, Egypt, coins were minted on which Nero assumed the same importance as the city's local god. After A.D. 65, even some coins from Rome began to show Nero wearing the crown previously used only for the deified emperors. Nero himself, who was never particularly attracted to any one deity for long, may simply have liked the coins' identification with the Greek god Apollo Citharoedus — Apollo the Lyre Player. However, the Romans were sensitive to such symbols, and it seemed to the senators that Nero, like Caligula, wanted to legitimize his absolute rule with a divinity he did not deserve.

Nero had continued to use the excuse of the Pisonian conspiracy to get rid of anyone he considered troublesome, and treason trials went on with a vengeance. Helping Nero to maintain his power was Tigellinus, who had instituted a network of informers. Anyone who offered the least pretext to an informer was accused of treason and sentenced to die; his estates were then confiscated. Senators and equestrians, in order to protect their families from both the greed and the political persecution of the emperor, made sure they praised Nero in their wills, leaving him a large portion of their fortunes. Nero collected a great deal of money this way.

Nero forced into exile the prominent lawyer Gaius Cassius Longinus because he kept a bust of his ancestor Cassius, one of the assassins of Nero's ancestor Julius Caesar. The emperor had the entire family of Lucius Antitius — Rubellius Plautus's father-in-law — commit suicide because they hated him for killing Plautus. Lucan's father, Annaeus Mela, also accused of conspiracy, was forced to kill himself. In A.D. 66, the poet and satirist Petronius, dubbed Nero's *arbiter elegantiae* — judge of elegance — by Tacitus, became a victim of the terror. Petronius, the emperor's former drinking and banquet companion, is generally held to be the author of the *Satyricon*, a satirical Roman romance in prose and verse. Petronius incurred the jealousy of Tigellinus and was charged with being a friend of Scaevinus, one of the main Pisonian conspirators. It is reported that unlike most of those forced to commit suicide, Petronius denounced Nero's abominable behavior in a scathing passage in his will.

In a Roman funeral, bearers carry the deceased, accompanied by the family (top left) and other mourners. To ensure that their estates were not confiscated, wealthy Romans left a large legacy — in essence, a bribe — to Nero in their wills.

This bronze statuette of an actor dates from Roman imperial times. Nero continued his love affair with the theater, to the great amusement and delight of the plebs, who were fascinated with the thought of their emperor performing with common artists.

At last Nero brought down the man who had long been a thorn in his side — the conscientious senator Thrasea Paetus. Thrasea, protesting Nero's excesses and disgusted by the Senate's servile behavior, had stopped attending most sessions. A long list of charges was prepared against Thrasea, including his refusal to honor the divine Poppaea and dereliction of duty at the Senate, but his real crime was simply that he opposed everything Nero did. Thrasea was charged with lack of allegiance and the setting of a bad example in the Senate.

Thrasea met his end with his customary dignity. The Senate's death verdict reached him when he was with friends, discussing the nature of the soul. He immediately urged his companions to leave, fearing they would be contaminated by his fall from grace. He remained to the end a staunch adherent of the Stoic principles of dignity and strength. Tacitus states that he died nobly to provide an example of fortitude for coming generations. With the death of Thrasea, the last of the truly virtuous Roman senators had been silenced. Nero had frightened the senators into complete obedience.

The same year that Thrasea died, Nero celebrated in his grand, crowd-pleasing fashion the arrival of Tiridates, who had traveled to Italy to be crowned king of Armenia by Nero. Dio Cassius reports that Tiridates' journey west was paid for by Rome. In the early summer Tiridates met Nero in Naples, and together they rode to Rome. Nero entered the capital in a military triumphal progress and proceeded to put on the greatest public show of his reign.

For the coronation ceremony to be held at the Forum, Nero donned the gold-embroidered purple toga of the *triumphator*, or military victor. Surrounding the temples of the Forum were praetorian guards in full armor, and the people of Rome watched from the rooftops and cheered. Nero waited as Tiridates came up the Via Sacra (the Sacred Road), which was lined with soldiers to honor the king. After prostrating himself before Nero, Tiridates was crowned, and Nero, in a grand gesture, ordered the doors of the Temple of Janus closed, a

symbol that peace reigned throughout the entire empire. Then the festivities began. Nero had a carnival put on for the people and took King Tiridates to watch performances in a theater the inside of which had been covered in gold. After the spectacle was over, Tiridates was given a substantial sum of money and sent back to his capital, Artaxata, now to be called Neroneia.

At the end of the year, Nero decided to fulfill an old ambition by touring Greece. This desire was a logical outcome of the love Nero had long held for all things Greek, but the Romans were dismayed by the trip for several reasons. They disliked Nero's infatuation with Greek culture and were apprehensive about the absence of the emperor from the capital. In addition they resented the person Nero left in charge, a freedman named Helius.

Nero was not the only emperor to admire the Greeks. Augustus and Claudius had both liked Greek literature. Indeed, Claudius, a scholar, was fluent in the language and wrote histories in Greek. Caligula had a great admiration for Greek culture. Nero's grandfather Germanicus, who wrote in Greek and translated Greek into Latin, had toured the country. Many upper-class Romans completed their education by attending the famous schools of rhetoric in Athens and on the island of Rhodes. Nero's

One of Nero's favorite stage characters was Orestes, a figure from Greek mythology shown here with his friend Pilades. In revenge for his father's death, Orestes murdered his own mother. The irony was not lost on the Romans.

This head of a charioteer comes from the sacred Greek city of Delphi. In A.D. 66 Nero went to Greece to participate in the national games. To please the emperor, the Greeks held all the games in that year and awarded him prizes for whatever he did.

interest in Greece stemmed from his artistic leanings. He envied the unfettered bohemian life of the Greek stage performers. His favorite performances were all of well-known figures from Greek plays or tales such as Orestes, Oedipus, and Hercules. He became a collector of Greek art, stationing agents in the provinces of Asia and Achaea (the name of the Roman province of Greece) to plunder many of the ancient sites for statues and sculptures. Pausanius, a Greek writer of the 2nd century A.D., states that Nero's agents removed 500 artworks from the city of Delphi alone.

Sometime in the autumn of A.D. 66 Nero left for Greece with a group of senators, the praetorian guards under Tigellinus, and the Augustiani. He demanded that the four great national games of Greece — Olympian, Delphic, Isthmian, and Nemean — all be held during his visit so that he could participate in each one. Although these contests were traditionally confined to athletics, the organizers wisely added musical competitions to the program. Nero was given prizes for whatever he did; even for those contests he did not take part in. Finally, like the fabled Greek kings he loved, Nero drove a 10-horse chariot. In one contest he fell out onto the racecourse and had to be helped to his feet. He failed to finish the race but nevertheless took first prize.

Nero was deeply serious about his stage performances. His dedication is recorded by Suetonius: "During the competitions he strictly observed the rules, never daring to clear his throat and even using his arm to wipe the sweat from his brow. [Handkerchiefs were not allowed.] Once, while acting in a tragedy, he dropped his scepter and quickly recovered it, but was terrified of disqualification. The accompanist, however . . . swore that the slip had passed unnoticed, because the audience was listening with such rapt attention; so he took heart again."

Toward the end of A.D. 66, Nero's visit to Greece was marred by the news of a rebellion in the Roman province of Judaea. To the Romans, the First Jewish Revolt, although serious, was just one of many

conflicts and so commanded no more attention than other rebellions; it was, however, a crucial event in Jewish history.

To most Romans Judaea was a small, almost worthless place, filled with incomprehensible, sullen subjects. Emperor Augustus had made the area an equestrian province; that is, it was ruled by a governor from the equestrian class. (The most important provinces were imperial and senatorial.) The governor of Judaea, who was called a procurator, maintained only a small army garrison, and assignment to Judaea was often looked upon by officials and soldiers as a punishment; there they could not accrue the riches or enjoy the sophistication found in other eastern provinces. On top of that, the inhabitants of the region bitterly resented the Roman presence.

The Jews occupied a special place in the Roman Empire. They were the only people who managed to gain exemptions from standard Roman provincial policies. Although they were baffled by the Jews' insistence on worshiping only one god, the Romans recognized the special nature of the Jewish religion and the central place it held in the lives of the Jews. The Jews were exempt from Roman military service. Perhaps even more surprising is that Rome allowed the Jews living in other provinces to send contributions — not to the treasury at Rome — but to the temple in Jerusalem.

In spite of these concessions, the Romans were thoroughly despised by most Jews in Judaea, who longed for the day of Jewish independence. Harsh economic and social divisions contributed to the constant tension between the ruling Romans and the Jews. Roman administrative officials made blunder after blunder in their dealings with the Jews, often offending them. Emperor Caligula had nearly started a war when he tried to get a statue of himself placed in the Jerusalem temple. Fortunately, he died before the idea was addressed.

In May A.D. 66, the procurator, in financial straits, appropriated some money from the Jerusalem temple. Outraged by this violation of the temple, the

A detail from the Arch of Titus shows Romans plundering the temple in Jerusalem. The Jewish revolt in late A.D. 66 was of only passing concern to Nero, but its suppression by the Romans, which culminated in the destruction of the temple, was a crucial event in Jewish history.

Jews rioted. When the governor permitted the local Roman troops to plunder a part of the city, the rioting grew furious. In August the required official sacrifice to Rome and the emperor was rejected by the temple priesthood. The Roman garrisons in Jerusalem and at the hilltop fortress of Masada, on the western shore of the Dead Sea, were slaughtered. The rioting spread throughout Jewish communities in the east; in Caesarea (a coastal town northwest of Jerusalem), long the site of tension between the Jews and the local Greek community, 20,000 Jews were killed. Rome was finally forced to address the problem as fighting worsened in several places.

As always, Nero remained uninterested in military matters. He found the Jewish revolt particularly inconvenient because he was in the midst of his Greek tour, an event he considered too important to be interrupted. The emperor created a separate command for the Jewish conflict and sent most of the Roman army in Syria to Judaea. In February A.D. 67, Nero appointed Vespasian commander of this army; together with his son Titus (Titus Flavius Vespasianus), Vespasian led an army of perhaps 50,000 men. In a long, tough war of attrition against a fierce Jewish resistance that belied its numbers, Vespasian and Titus reduced city after city.

The Jewish war would be held up for two years by the death of Nero and the subsequent political insecurity it created. Four years after the start of the war, Titus would conquer Jerusalem, sacking the city after a four-month siege. The temple would be destroyed and the Sanhedrin — the council of high priests — abolished. The devastation wrought to both life and property was enormous, but it was the loss of the temple — the religious center and the national focus of Jews throughout the empire — that affected the Jews the most. Its destruction signaled the end of the Jews' privileged position in the empire. From then on, contributions went to the temple of Jupiter Capitolinus in Rome.

After appointing Vespasian to deal with the Jewish war, Nero resumed his artistic activities in Greece. The emperor had thoroughly enjoyed himself during his trip, winning (to the surprise of no one) first prizes for all his performances. The climax of the imperial tour came in November A.D. 67, at the Isthmian Games at Corinth. In a grand, melodramatic gesture, Nero announced that he was restoring freedom to the Greeks. The proclamation survives on an inscription in Karditza, Greece: "Men of Hellas [Greece], I give you an unlooked for gift — if indeed anything may not be hoped for from one of my greatness of mind — a gift so great, you were incapable of asking for it. All Greeks inhabiting Achaea and the land called till now the Peloponnese receive freedom and immunity from taxes. . . ."

Granting "freedom" to a province did not mean that it was no longer subject to Rome; however, the former senatorial province would now be governed by a native Greek. Furthermore, immunity from the heavy Roman taxes was no small benefit — very few places enjoyed such a privilege. In Greece, the birthplace of democracy, freedom was a powerful word, and despite the dramatic posturing, Nero's declaration endeared him to the Greeks. Long after Nero was dead, the Greeks remembered this gesture with respect and affection.

While Nero was in Greece, disaffection with his rule had been growing. He had alienated the upper

On a Greek vase, Nike (Victory) crowns a charioteer. Nero, convinced that he had won his contests by sheer talent, proudly displayed to the disgusted Romans the hundreds of laurel wreaths he was awarded by the Greeks.

classes by leaving his freedman, Helius, in charge and giving him all the powers of the emperor over life and death. Reports were circulating that Nero's mistress, Calvia Crispinilla, was involved in making government decisions. The heretofore servile Senate was growing increasingly unwilling to tolerate such a situation. When minor rebellions broke out in various parts of the empire — a good indication that central authority was disintegrating — Helius sent word to Nero that his presence in the capital was urgently required. Nero's responses to Helius's messages were irresponsible; he was simply having too good a time in Greece to be bothered with the business of government. Nero had let Roman politics slip from his hand, and the Senate would be quick to take advantage of his mistake.

When a grain shortage caused by the increased financial demands of Nero's Greek tour and the revolt in Judaea threatened Rome, Helius became desperate. Despite their love of Nero's entertainments, the Roman plebs would turn on him in a minute if they could not get their bread; riots over grain shortages were common occurrences in Roman history, dating back to republican days. Helius was forced to hurry to Greece to convince Nero of the seriousness of the ugly mood in Rome. The emperor finally and reluctantly agreed to return.

Before leaving Greece, Nero displayed an unbridled generosity. He gave presents of gold pieces to contest judges and Roman citizenship to all inhabitants of the Greek cities in which he had competed. When Nero returned to Italy in January A.D. 68, he carried with him nearly 2,000 laurel wreaths for his Greek victories. He landed at Naples, and like a victorious general, he entered in a triumphal procession, which he repeated twice — in Antium, his birthplace, and in Alba Longa, the legendary site of Rome's beginnings — before proceeding to the capital in Augustus's triumphal chariot. Wearing a Greek cloak, a purple robe flecked with gold stars, and the Olympic crown atop his long yellow curls, he was preceded by youths carrying placards that bore not the names of cities he had conquered but

In a Roman triumph, victorious soldiers march through the capital city. Nero's triumph, held for his theatrical exploits in Greece, was an obscene insult to the Senate and, more importantly, to the Roman army.

of the contests he had won. Big Roman letters described his competitors and the songs he had sung to defeat them. Military victors were normally followed by their legions, but Nero was escorted by the Augustiani, acting every bit like conquering soldiers. Although the senators were disgusted, the Roman plebs, roaring with applause, lined his route from the Circus to the Forum and the Temple of Apollo on the Palatine hill and showered their emperor with flowers. This procession would be Nero's last magnificent spectacle.

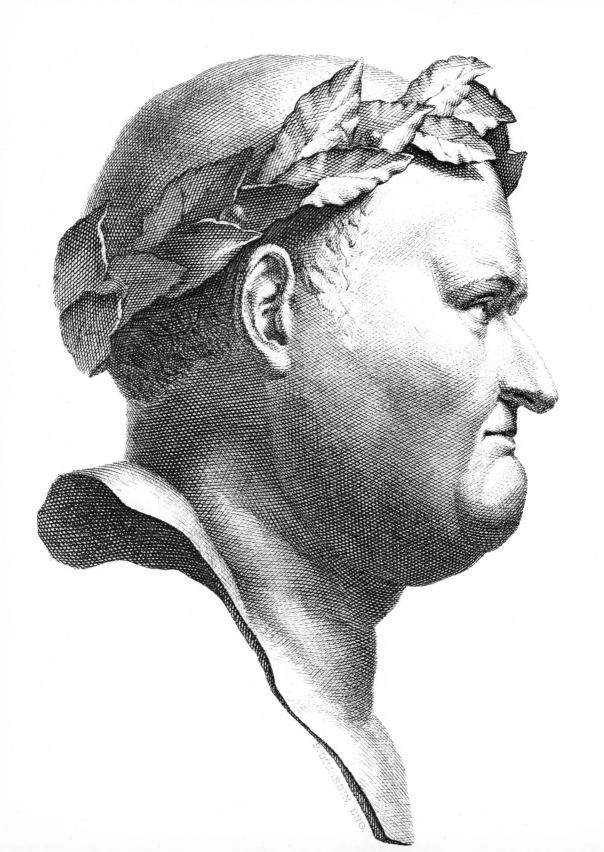

9

The End of Nero Caesar

Helius's frantic summonses to Nero in Greece may have been based on more than just civil discontent, for while Nero was abroad, another conspiracy to replace him had been brewing. During Nero's sojourn, persecution of members of the upper classes continued in Rome, and the emperor himself was responsible for the deaths of a number of prominent men.

Not much is known about the Vinician conspiracy of late A.D. 66–early 67. It apparently took its name from Annius Vinicianus, the son-in-law of the great general, Corbulo, and it has been suggested that the conspirators meant to replace Nero with Corbulo. In any event, because of the familial connection, Corbulo came under suspicion, and sometime in early A.D. 67, Nero summoned Corbulo to Greece, where the respected commander was forced to commit suicide. Nero then sent for the governors of the provinces of Germania Superior and Germania Inferior (Upper and Lower Germany), Scribonius Rufus and Scribonius Proculus, and the brothers were also commanded to kill themselves. Their crime is

In [Nero's] history one discerns the outstanding weakness of a hereditary system; men with neither character nor experience can come to positions of absolute power.
—ALLAN MASSIE
British historian,
on Nero's historical
example

Vespasian, whom Nero sent to quell the rebellion in Judaea, was a simple, practical military man. After the tumult caused by Nero's death, Vespasian became the first ruler of the succeeding dynasty, the Flavians. He brought to the throne honesty and common sense, traits that Nero had lacked.

The Roman port of Ostia was one of the beneficiaries of Nero's grand construction projects. Combined with the ostentatious spectacles the emperor put on, his building escapades severely strained the Roman treasury.

unknown, but Nero may have reasoned that given Corbulo's example, the provincial governors, who had legions at their command, might revolt against him. In his fear of the old, established noble families, whose bloodlines were equally impressive as his own, Nero thought that men of more modest backgrounds would be less threatening in provincial command posts, and he promoted a number of such men, including Vespasian, who was born in Spain.

Nero must have been out of touch with the mood of the two groups he could not now afford to alienate: the plebs and the soldiers. His absolute power was ultimately tied up in his control of the army, but the common soldier saw only an emperor whose main interests were in keeping himself entertained. What was worse, he appeared on the stage like a Greek actor; behavior the legionaries considered undignified. As B. H. Warmington, a biographer of Nero put it, "The Roman rabble might love Nero for the lavishness of his entertainments but the Roman soldier despised him for his indolence [laziness]."

Nero's activities in Greece were well known to the armies stationed in the east, and when the emperor rid himself of Corbulo and the governors of Ger-

many, nervous Roman commanders throughout the empire began to court the loyalty of their own legions. Once the Roman troops accepted the idea that their first loyalty was to their immediate commanders and not to the emperor, Nero's fate was sealed.

Both Nero's trip to Greece and the major rebellion in Judaea had caused shortages of money and grain in Rome. Nero had been draining the imperial treasury for years to finance grand building projects. In addition to the Golden House, Nero had started the construction of a new harbor at the Italian port of Ostia; a canal to drain the Tiber River below Rome; and another canal to cut through the Isthmus of Corinth. Nero's massive projects had also included a triumphal arch to celebrate Corbulo's military victories in the east; the Macellum Magnum — the Great Market — on the Caelian hill in Rome; several Greek-style gymnasia in which to hold athletic contests; and the Thermae Neronianae — Nero's Baths — a huge public bath in Rome. The many spectacles and public entertainments the emperor held in Rome also contributed to the disastrous financial situation of Nero's later years.

Finally, most Romans were appalled by the emperor's lack of interest in actually ruling, his artistic leanings, and his growing inclination to see himself as a semidivine ruler like the Egyptian god-kings of old. The stage was set for the final performance. The leading actors would enter from the wings to claim center stage.

In March A.D. 68 Gaius Julius Vindex, a native Gaul and the governor of Gallia Lugdunensis (modern central France), approached several provincial military men to back a revolt against Nero. Vindex, with no legions of his own, asked Servius Sulpicius Galba, the governor of Hispania Tarraconensis (northern and central modern Spain), to lead the revolt.

Vindex, who had the reputation of being a courageous and intelligent man, won support among several powerful Gallic tribes and some Roman cities established in Gaul, but he by no means held complete control over the province. Rival tribes and a number of towns, including Lugdunum (the modern French city of Lyon), opposed him. Galba, who was 72 at the time, came from a very distinguished Roman republican family and had held many important posts, including praetor, consul, and governor of several provinces. Galba tallied his potential support. He could probably count on the backing of Seneca's family in Spain, but as far as troops went, Galba had only one legion under his command. He chose not to act immediately.

Nero was enjoying himself in Naples when word of Vindex's revolt reached him. Either he could not stir himself to take it seriously, or his head was still too full of his Greek victories to act on the information. Instead, he went to the gymnasium every day and watched the athletic contests. It did not occur to Nero that the Roman plebs, after all the games and shows he had provided for them, would fail to back him. Even at this point, Nero still commanded the loyalty of several legions and might have saved himself had he been decisive enough to appeal to them. As far as Nero knew the praetorian guard continued to be loyal, and anyone who was backed by the guard controlled Rome.

Vindex continued to issue edicts against Nero, denouncing his extravagances. Suetonius reports that what most ruffled Nero was Vindex's insulting charge that the emperor was a bad lyre player. Nero's only action at this point was to send a letter to the Senate, asking it to avenge him against Vindex. Finally, he was persuaded to return to Rome. But when his advisers tried to discuss the threat from Gaul with him, he seemed more eager to demonstrate his new musical instrument—a water organ.

In early April A.D. 68, Galba threw in his lot with Vindex, perhaps reasoning that by now he would be accused of treason anyway. His legion proclaimed him emperor at Carthago Nova (Cartagena, Spain), and he received the immediate support of an old enemy of Nero; Salvius Otho, Poppaea's former husband and the governor of Lusitania. It was at this point that Nero began to react to the threat. He called in legions from other provinces, and at the end of April he announced he would be the sole consul, a traditional sign of an emergency at Rome. Yet Nero continued to live his life of luxury, giving lavish banquets at which he sang bawdy songs about the Gallic revolt.

The standard issue of a Roman legionary included swords, helmets, shields, and body armor. When rebellion broke out in Gaul, Nero at first refused to believe he had lost the support of the army and did not move quickly enough to suppress the revolt.

Servius Sulpicius Galba, governor of Spain, was a vigorous, efficient, and highly respected veteran. When he threw his support to the rebels, Nero finally realized the seriousness of his situation.

According to Suetonius, Nero dreamed up several fantastic schemes to deal with the growing rebellion. (It is important to note that Tacitus's work on this period did not survive; modern scholarship must rely on Suetonius, who is considered less reliable, and on the fragments of Dio Cassius.) One of Nero's ideas was to depose and execute all army commanders and provincial governors. He also contemplated poisoning the entire Senate at a banquet. Then he spoke of traveling with his armies to Gaul, where he would fall as a suppliant before the Gallic troops and weep, a gesture, he felt, sure to touch their hearts and win back their loyalty. His head was filled with the songs he would compose to commemorate the joyful occasion. The emperor locked himself in his palace while Rome seethed with excitement.

Vindex began his campaign with a siege of Lugdunum, but he had only one legion, most of which was made up of Gallic auxiliaries. In May the governor of Germania Superior, Verginius Rufus, who had been waiting to see if Vindex was successful, decided to back the emperor, and at Vesontio (Besançon, France) Verginius's three Roman legions, with superior arms and training, massacred 20,000 of Vindex's men. Vindex committed suicide. The troops from Germany, flushed with victory, proposed to make their commander the new emperor; it is reported that Verginius refused. When Galba, still in Spain, heard the news, he sent a message to

Verginius asking him to join his cause against Nero, then he took refuge in the Spanish interior. It seemed as if the revolt would die out on its own.

But the provincials did not give up, and Nero's enemies in Rome were waiting for the right opportunity to depose him. Had Nero at this point taken control of the armies he had summoned to Rome for aid; had he moved swiftly and decisively against Galba, Otho, and the other provincial officials and commanders involved in the revolt, he might have saved his empire. However, all he could do was propose wild schemes and bemoan his fate.

It is unclear why, but Tigellinus seems to have played no role in Nero's last months. Instead, it was the other praetorian commander, Nymphidius Sabinus, who reached an agreement with the Senate and convinced the guard to defect. Once Nero lost the support of the praetorians, he lost Rome. Suetonius writes that Nero had Locusta provide him

The Roman historian Tacitus left a record of much of Nero's reign, but most of the section dealing with events of the emperor's final year did not survive. Students of Nero have had to rely on less reliable or fragmentary works for details of Nero's last days.

with a fatal poison. On June 8 Nero fled the city, perhaps intending to travel to Egypt, where he said he would make his living as a lyre player. The praetorian guard under Sabinus declared for Galba, and the Senate pronounced Nero a public enemy. The once-adored emperor of Rome was now a hunted criminal.

Nero set out, his face covered to avoid recognition, for a Roman suburban villa owned by one of his freedmen, Phaon. Four of his former slaves, the only companions he now had, accompanied him. On the way a small earthquake and lightning frightened him as evil omens, and he was equally alarmed when he heard people talking excitedly of Galba and of the hunt for the emperor.

Suetonius poignantly describes his arrival at his hideout: "Then he pulled out all the thorns from his ragged cloak and crawled into the villa by way of the tunnel. In the first room he came to, he sank down on a couch with a poor mattress over which an old cape had been thrown and, although hungry, refused some coarse bread offered him. . . ."

The praetorian guard was the key element in the fall of Nero. When these soldiers, who resented taking orders from Nero's lackeys, defected to the side of Galba, the military turned against Nero, sealing his fate.

He ordered his companions to dig a grave for him, to be decorated with any pieces of marble they could find. A runner arrived and informed him of the Senate's decision to punish him "in ancient style": With his head held in a wooden fork, he would be flogged to death with rods. Nero, pacing the rooms, examined the daggers he had carried with him, but he flinched from suicide, unlike his Stoic opponents who had regarded it as the simplest of duties. "How ugly and vulgar my life has become!" he cried. Bewailing his fate, he lamented, "What an artist perishes in me!" When he heard the galloping horses of the soldiers come to arrest him, he persuaded one of his freedmen to help him stab himself in the throat and soon died. Nero was 31 years old.

Otho is proclaimed emperor by his troops in January A.D. 69. Galba succeeded Nero, but civil war ensued when Otho, Galba's former ally, killed the aged emperor and several men vied for power.

The new emperor, Galba, permitted Nero's nurses and his former mistress Acte to bury him with an expensive funeral at the ancestral tomb of Nero's family clan, the Domitii. When he arrived in Rome in October, Galba immediately caused trouble by killing some soldiers who had come out to meet him, and he refused to give the lavish donatives the army was accustomed to receiving on the accession of a new emperor. In all, he alienated too many people, and provincial revolts broke out anew the following January. In mid-January, Otho brutally murdered Galba to make himself ruler. Thus began the political turmoil and civil strife of the period known as the Year of the Four Emperors. Not until the accession of Emperor Vespasian, the founder of the Flavian dynasty, at the end of A.D. 69, was order restored in the empire.

With Nero's death the Julio-Claudian line came to an end. Men who had ties to the attitudes and traditions of the old Roman Republic were dying out; a new stage in imperial Rome was beginning. A legend sprang up around Nero that he had escaped and would return; before the end of the century, three pretenders would appear, each claiming to be Nero. In the early Christian literature the return of Nero is seen as the appearance of the Antichrist, signaling the approach of the end of the world. However, it seemed that many regretted Nero's death, especially in Greece and the east, and in view of the subsequent conflicts they longed for the relative peace his reign had provided. For years flowers were put on his tomb and images of him were displayed in public.

According to the tradition established by Augustus, the emperor was no more than the *princeps* — the first citizen of Rome. From early in Nero's life, however, it can be seen that the obligations and duties inherent in the concept of *princeps* did not hold much interest for him. His early successes as emperor testify more to his youth and the influence of stronger men than to any desire on his part to run the empire well. Once he began to revel in his own power, the only aspects of empire that interested him were the ones that allowed him to fulfill

When Nero inherited the imperial authority, he was too young to distinguish between power and privilege. His temperament was ill suited to governing, and his overindulgences led him into the depravity that was his ultimate downfall.

his personal ambitions of glory. As Warmington writes, "It was not so much the cruelty as the frivolity and ineptitude of Nero which led to his downfall."

Suetonius says of Nero, "His dominant characteristics were his thirst for popularity and his jealousy of men who caught the public eye." Those traits can be traced to his massive insecurity, fostered in the treacherous circumstances of the imperial circle in which he grew up, and his conception of himself as an artist. An artist must have license, license of the imagination, but it must be combined with habits of discipline. As emperor, Nero was given unlimited license over other men's lives, but he was never required to act with discipline. It was a powerful, fatal blend.

Further Reading

Cunliffe, Barry. *Rome and Her Empire.* New York: McGraw-Hill, 1978.

Grant, Michael. *Emperor in Revolt: Nero.* New York: American Heritage, 1970.

Griffin Miriam T. *Nero: The End of a Dynasty.* New Haven: Yale University Press, 1984.

Massie, Allan. *The Caesars.* London: Secker and Warburg, 1983.

Suetonius. *The Twelve Caesars.* Revised and translated by Robert Graves. New York: Penguin Books, 1983.

Tacitus. *The Annals of Imperial Rome.* Translated by Michael Grant. New York: Penguin Books, 1985.

Chronology

Dec. 15, A.D. 37	Born Lucius Domitius Ahenobarbus
39	Nero's mother, Agrippina the Younger, exiled by Emperor Caligula; Nero raised by aunt
41	Agrippina recalled by Emperor Claudius
49	Claudius marries Agrippina Philosopher Seneca appointed Nero's tutor
50	Claudius formally adopts Nero
53	Nero marries Octavia, daughter of Claudius
54	Becomes emperor after Agrippina poisons Claudius
58	Parthian War begins
59	Nero institutes Juvenalia celebration Orders murder of Agrippina
60	Holds first Neronian games
61	The Iceni, led by Boudicca, revolt in Britain
62	Seneca loses influence over Nero and retires Nero orders death of Octavia; marries Poppaea
64	Great Fire ravages Rome; Nero blamed for fire and persecutes Christians as scapegoats; begins construction of Golden House Makes first appearance on public stage in Naples
65	Pisonian conspiracy to oust Nero fails, results in purge of senatorial class; Seneca forced to commit suicide Nero competes in second Neronian games Kills Poppaea in a fit of anger
66	Crowns Tiridates king of Armenia Travels to Greece to participate in national games Jewish War begins; Nero sends Vespasian to Judea
68	Vindex revolts in Gaul; Galba takes up rebellion in Spain
June 9, 68	Declared a state enemy, Nero commits suicide

Index

Elizabeth Powers is a novelist and short-story writer based in New York City.

Arthur M. Schlesinger, jr., taught history at Harvard for many years and is currently Albert Schweitzer Professor of the Humanities at City University of New York. He is the author of numerous highly praised works in American history and has twice been awarded the Pulitzer Prize. He served in the White House as special assistant to Presidents Kennedy and Johnson.

PICTURE CREDITS